Choosing the Kingdom

To Peggy –

Who knows deeply what it is to
glimpse and choose the reign of God in
daily life –

Choosing the Kingdom

Missional Preaching for the
Household of God

John Addison Dally

THE
ALBAN
INSTITUTE

Herndon, Virginia
www.alban.org

The Alban Institute
2121 Cooperative Way, Suite 100
Herndon, VA 20171

Unless otherwise noted, all Scripture quotations are from the New Revised Standard Version of the Bible, copyright © 1989, Division of Christian Education of the National Council of the Churches of Christ in the United States of America, and are used by permission.

Cover design by Tobias Becker.

Library of Congress Cataloging-in-Publication Data

Dally, John Addison.
  Choosing the kingdom : missional preaching for the household of God / John Addison Dally.
      p. cm. — (The vital worship, healthy congregations series)
  Includes bibliographical references.
  ISBN 978-1-56699-359-3
  1. Church renewal. 2. Mission of the church. 3. Church. 4. Missions—Theory. I. Title.

  BV600.3.D35 2007
  251—dc22

                                    2007045793

        12 11 10 09 08   VG   1 2 3 4 5

For Beth and all my students whose choice for the kingdom of God has significantly complicated their career plans.

Contents

Editor's Foreword

Healthy Congregations

Christianity is a "first-person plural" religion, where communal worship, service, fellowship, and learning are indispensable for grounding and forming individual faith. The strength of Christianity in North America depends on the presence of healthy, spiritually nourishing, well-functioning congregations. Congregations are the cradle of Christian faith, the communities in which children of all ages are supported, encouraged, and formed for lives of service. Congregations are the habitat in which the practices of the Christian life can flourish.

As living organisms, congregations are by definition in a constant state of change. Whether the changes are in membership, pastoral leadership, lay leadership, the needs of the community, or the broader culture, a crucial mark of healthy congregations is their ability to deal creatively and positively with change. The fast pace of change in contemporary culture, with its bias toward, not against, change only makes the challenge of negotiating change all the more pressing for congregations.

Vital Worship

At the center of many discussions about change in churches today is the topic of worship. This is not surprising, for worship is at the center of congregational life. To "go to church" means, for most members of congregations, "to go to worship." In *How Do We*

Worship?, Mark Chaves begins his analysis with the simple assertion, "Worship is the most central and public activity engaged
in by American religious congregations" (Alban Institute, 1999,
p. 1). Worship styles are one of the most significant reasons that
people choose to join a given congregation. Correspondingly, they
are central to the identity of most congregations.

Worship is also central on a much deeper level. Worship is the
locus of what several Christian traditions identify as the nourishing center of congregational life: preaching, common prayer, and
the celebration of ordinances or sacraments. Significantly, what
many traditions elevate to the status of "the means of grace" or
even the "marks of the church" are essentially liturgical actions.
Worship is central, most significantly, for theological reasons.
Worship both reflects and shapes a community's faith. It expresses
a congregation's view of God and enacts a congregation's relationship with God and each other.

We can identify several specific factors that contribute to spiritually vital worship and thereby strengthen congregational life.

- Congregations, and the leaders that serve them, need a
  shared vision for worship that is grounded in more than
  personal aesthetic tastes. This vision must draw on the
  deep theological resources of Scripture, the Christian tradition, and the unique history of the congregation.
- Congregational worship should be integrated with the
  whole life of the congregation. It can serve as the "source
  and summit" from which all the practices of the Christian life flow. Worship both reflects and shapes the life of
  the church in education, pastoral care, community service,
  fellowship, justice, hospitality, and every other aspect of
  church life.
- The best worship practices feature not only good worship
  "content," such as discerning sermons, honest prayers,
  creative artistic contributions, celebrative and meaningful
  rituals for baptism and the Lord's Supper. They also arise
  of out of good process, involving meaningful contributions
  from participants, thoughtful leadership, honest evalua-
  tion, and healthy communication among leaders.

Vital Worship, Healthy Congregations Series

The Vital Worship, Healthy Congregations Series is designed to reflect the kind of vibrant, creative energy and patient reflection that will promote worship that is both relevant and profound. It is designed to invite congregations to rediscover a common vision for worship, to sense how worship is related to all aspects of congregational life, and to imagine better ways of preparing both better "content" and better "process" related to the worship life of their own congregations.

It is important to note that strengthening congregational life through worship renewal is a delicate and challenging task precisely because of the uniqueness of each congregation. This book series is not designed to represent a single denomination, Christian tradition, or type of congregation. Nor is it designed to serve as arbiter of theological disputes about worship. Books in the series will note the significance of theological claims about worship, but they may, in fact, represent quite different theological visions from each other, or from our work at the Calvin Institute of Christian Worship. That is, the series is designed to call attention to instructive examples of congregational life and to explore these examples in ways that allow readers in very different communities to compare and contrast these examples with their own practice. The models described in any given book may for some readers be instructive as examples to follow. For others, a given example may remind them of something they are already doing well, or something they will choose not to follow because of theological commitments or community history.

Choosing the Kingdom: Missional Preaching for the Household of God confronts any approach to preaching that is content with the status quo or that assumes that that the church is merely an end in itself. In this prophetic mode, John Dally engages the growing literature on missional ecclesiology and probes it significance for the act of liturgical preaching. As you study this book, pay particular attention to its vivid awareness of divine activity. "Missional" must never be a code-word for "heroic human achievement in revitalizing churches." Rather, it is a call to cultivate a robust awareness of God's ongoing work of redemption, which is carried out in part through commissioning the church and its members. This approach fosters a season-of-Advent kind of piety that centers on expectation and hope and eagerly embraces divine commands to engage in life-tranforming work, not as onerous obligations but as generous gifts.

By promoting encounters with instructive examples from various parts of the body of Christ, we pray that these volumes will help leaders make good judgments about worship in their congregations and that, by the power of God's Spirit, these congregations will flourish.

John D. Witvliet
Calvin Institute for Christian Worship

Acknowledgments

I am deeply grateful to the Rev. Dr. Craig Satterlee, the Axel Jacob and Gerda Maria (Swanson) Carlson professor of homiletics at the Lutheran School of Theology at Chicago, for recommending this work to Alban Institute for publication, and to the superb editorial staff at Alban who brought it to completion with meticulous care and unfailing graciousness. I am equally grateful to the seven cohorts of students who have taken classes in missional preaching from me over the past five years. Their responses have profoundly shaped the content of this book.

Introduction

Every autumn I ask my beginning preaching students to go the library and survey English and American books about preaching from the late nineteenth century to the present to see what common themes they can detect. I give them a hint by suggesting that they can just look at the introduction of each book. It's not long before the students begin to notice a pattern. A significant proportion of books about preaching written in the past 150 years begin with some variation on this sentence:

Preaching today is facing a crisis.

By "today" the authors of these books may be speaking of contexts as different as the announcement of Darwin's theory of evolution, the advent of weapons of mass destruction in the First World War, the Great Depression, the dawn of the nuclear age, or the exodus from mainline churches in the 1960s and 1970s. The crisis they describe is more consistent: preaching is not finding an audience, or it is not transforming the audience it finds. The diagnosis for improvement varies in each decade, ranging from different approaches to exegesis to new ideas for sermon construction to better skills for public speaking. Exegesis, sermon construction, and delivery remain the stock-in-trade for those of us who teach preaching to this day, yet somehow the crisis continues despite all the suggested improvements. Like diet books, preaching books continue to sell on the premise that dramatic results are just weeks away.

Can this book be any different? Has the author not painted himself into a corner with his gross generalization about the nature of books on preaching? At least this broad-brush survey of the literature can suggest a way forward: rather than delineate the ramifications of "today" or "the crisis," it seems overdue to consider the nature of *preaching* itself. What the New Testament knew as proclamation (*keryssein*) became the teaching (*didache*) of the Constantinian Church, and persuasion and apologetics in the post-Enlightenment West. As recently as the 1960s, no less distinguished a theologian than Karl Rahner foresaw a Christian diaspora and a return to modest house communities by the late twentieth century—a reduction in scale that would have profoundly affected the shape of preaching had it happened. But Rahner and others of his stripe did not foresee the global resurgence of Christianity as a world religion in the late twentieth century as the seeds of Western colonialism bore unexpected fruit. Today the Christian faith is moving through one of the greatest sea changes in its two-thousand-year history, and we can no longer assume that we know exactly what kind of animal preaching is or ought to be.

"Sea change"? The notion itself is still news to many North American seminary professors, clergy, and people in the pews. Paradigm shifts are typically viewed best in hindsight; after all, no one alive in 1356 would have described herself as living in the "Middle Ages." Yet the collapse of Western imperial Christianity and the renewal of the understanding of mission that gave rise to the documents of the New Testament represent a shift in theology that can be glimpsed even as we move through it, however unknown its eventual implications might be. We are living with a foot in each of two worlds today. For many North American Christians, "mission" still connotes sending representatives of Western Christianity to the non-Western world, laden with crayons and vaccines. For others, the notion of becoming "missional" has completely transformed their sense of the church as an institution and their role in it. For these Christians, "mission" is no longer about an optional activity of the church but about participating in God's redeeming activity in a world bent on self-destruction.

Choosing the Kingdom will try to speak to both these audiences: tracing the sea change and its implications for preachers who have yet to encounter the word "missional" in their daily lives, and offering concrete suggestions for a reconception of the preaching task for those whose imaginations have already been captured by the possibilities inherent in a missional identity. We begin with defining the word "missional" itself—briefly, for those who already know it well.

CHAPTER 1

Missional: Is That a Word?

The word "missional" seems to follow the rules for forming adjectives in English (like "regional"), but it sounds odd to the ear nonetheless. It has yet to make it into the *Oxford English Dictionary*, in print or online,[1] and it isn't in any Webster's that I was able to peruse. You can find it in various online dictionary sites, but as of 2006, it has yet to break out of the cocoon of churchspeak. Is there really any need for it, even in theological circles? "Mission" already functions as an adjective, but it refers to a style of architecture emanating from eighteenth-century California. "Missionary" also serves as an adjective ("missionary zeal" or the perennially amusing "missionary position"), typically drained of any religious meaning. There's also "missiological," but that adjective refers to the academic discipline that studies mission, not to mission itself.

Although the word has not yet made the big-time dictionaries, a Web search for "missional" yields 864,000 hits, give or take a few thousand. About 800,000 of those entries seem to be defending the word's existence. Countless blog entries and e-zine articles begin with some version of "Why 'Missional' Is Not a Bad Word." So the word seems to be both widely used and widely resisted. Its etymology is even traced in various ways. Milfred Minatrea, author of *Shaped by God's Heart: The Passion and Practices of Missional Churches,* attributes the word to Charles Van Engen of Fuller Theological Seminary and says he began using the phrase "missional relationships" in 1991.[2] Others credit United Methodist Bishop Edsel Albert Ammons's *Congregational Linkage for*

Missional Ministry, published in 1975,[3] or even Robert E. Speer's 1919 book *The Gospel and the New World,*[4] a book that does not actually use the word "missional" but apparently implies it, a claim made by Anthony Bradley in the same installment of his blog cited above. Regardless of the word's true pedigree, there is no doubt that it came into widespread usage in mainline North American (and global English-speaking) Christianity with the publication of *Missional Church*[5] by the theologians of the Gospel and Our Culture Network in 1998.[6] Interestingly, this book defines the word "ecclesial" for its readers but never does the same for the word "missional," though it provides a thick description of what it means:

> [The] ecclesiocentric understanding of mission has been replaced during this century by a profoundly theocentric reconceptualization of Christian mission. We have come to see that mission is not merely an activity of the church. Rather, mission is the result of God's initiative, rooted in God's purposes to restore and heal creation. "Mission" means "sending," and it is the central biblical theme describing the purpose of God's action in human history . . . [Our] challenge today is to move from church with mission to missional church.[7]

Not only the definition but also the spirit and approach of *Missional Church* will be the jumping-off point for this book. The renewed vision of a "sent" church that fills the multiple volumes of the Gospel and Our Culture Network's publications since 1998 is both rich and deep, but to date the authors have not explored the implications of their work for preaching except in some brief and passing references. Nevertheless, their championing of the word "missional" has a great deal of history behind it, a lineage worth understanding. "Missional" is a word that is here to stay, a word with vast implications for the future of the church.

They Told Us So

The key thinkers of the rebirth of Christian missiology in the late twentieth century laid the foundations for missional theology a hundred years before there was a Gospel and Our Culture Network. Roland Allen (1868-1947), Anglican missionary to China, Africa, and, in the deepest sense, his own native England, witnessed firsthand the hollowness of the Church of England at home and abroad, even as he testified to the power of the Holy Spirit to gather indigenous Christian communities throughout the globe, communities shaped in the locally empowered pattern used by the apostle Paul. Filled with zeal to serve as a missionary sent by the church to the non-Christian peoples of the world, Allen came to believe that the professionalization of the clergy and the cultural chauvinism embedded in most of the theology he was expected to represent proved to be greater hindrances than even his very effective ministry with native peoples could surmount. Returning to England, he found less faith in the gathered Christian community than he had experienced in non-Christian China; men and women participated in the sacramental and liturgical life of the church with no real expectation that the promises of Christianity were either true or useful to their lives. Allen wrote extensively on the need for locally ordained, voluntary clergy raised up within local communities, on the scandal of disunity among Christian denominations that all invoke the Holy Spirit, and on the autonomy of indigenous churches. Few paid any attention to these ideas during Allen's lifetime; indeed, he once told his grandson that he was welcome to read any of the books Allen had written, "but I don't think anyone's going to understand them until I've been dead ten years."[8]

Someone who did understand Allen's writings, indeed, the one who made them *lingua franca* in a reborn vision of Christian mission, was Lesslie Newbigin (1909-1998), bishop in the Church of South India. Following a similar curriculum vitae, Newbigin began his professional life as an ordained Presbyterian minister sent from England by his church to be a missionary in India. There he learned the truth of Allen's assertion that what had passed unchallenged as the proclamation of the gospel for centuries was so thoroughly wrapped in the mantle of Western European culture that it had become a pernicious message of submission at its worst or, at its most benign, a tepid glass of sherry offered to people who would prefer to drink something else. Taking Allen's thought a step further, Newbigin began to speak and write about a new kind of missionary: one faithful to the *missio Dei*, God's sending, rather than one sent by the institutional church. And Newbigin made the forceful case that those who told the story of God's sending—of the prophets, the Christ, and the Holy Spirit—needed to become conversant in the realities of a pluralist society in which Christianity could no longer claim pride of place on the basis of imperial power. As associate general secretary of the World Council of Churches' Division of World Mission and Evangelism, Newbigin had an effective bully pulpit, and his theology of mission received wide notice and debate among the world's Christians.

Unlike Allen and Newbigin, David J. Bosch (1929-1992) was not a missionary sent to Asia by an English Church. Indeed, born into a family of Afrikaner farmers in South Africa, he was brought up to despise the English and to ignore the blacks who were native to the place he called home. Like Allen and Newbigin, however, Bosch was deeply influenced by the student evangelical fellowship he joined in college. Through that involvement Bosch realized three forms of call: to the ordained ministry of the Dutch Reformed Church, to the life of a missionary, and to speaking and working for the overturning of the apartheid system that his own parents' political party had made the law of the land in 1948 as he was entering college. After doctoral work in Switzerland (a thesis on mission and eschatology in the New Testament), Bosch returned to work as a missionary and church planter for seven years among the Xhosa people of the Transkei. Thus, like Allen and Newbigin before him, this future leading light of a reformed missiology developed his thought in the real world of Christian communities striving to become faithful in the wake of Christian imperialism.

Teaching first on the faculty of a small seminary in the Transkei, Bosch eventually accepted a post as professor of missiology at the University of South Africa in Pretoria. It was there, in 1991, that he produced his magisterial *Transforming Mission*, described by Newbigin as "a kind of Summa Missiologica," tracing as it does the development of the *missio Dei* from the ministry of Jesus and the writing of the New Testament all the way to the late twentieth century. Its wide-angle view of the church in history gave impetus to the growing awareness that the whole church, fragmented and divided by nationalism and self-interest, might be entering upon a new era of faithfulness to the original message of Jesus and his apostolic interpreters. Twice offered a post at Princeton Theological Seminary, Bosch remained committed to the battle against apartheid and its effects on South Africa until his death in an automobile accident in 1992.

From Sending to Being Sent

Each of these pastors, missionaries, and theologians contributed to the renewal of a New Testament sense of the *missio Dei* that swept throughout the global church during the twentieth century and generated the sea change in Christian theology alluded to earlier in this chapter. While each of these men was profoundly formed by the Western European expression of Christianity, the desire to understand the implications of God's sending led all three into multicultural dialogue and political conflict with their ordaining churches when their calls for reform could no longer be ignored.

In the 1980s the Gospel and Our Culture Network (GOCN) took shape in the United States and Canada in response to the Gospel and Culture discussions that sprang up in Great Britain after the publication of Lesslie Newbigin's *The Other Side of 1984: Questions for the Churches.* An interdenominational group of scholars and theologians, GOCN summed up the emerging consensus in its first book-length publication, *Missional Church: A Vision for the Sending of the Church in North America,* in 1998. The title of its first chapter describes the arrival of its new/old gospel: "From Sending to Being Sent." Mission in the New Testament is not an activity of the church but an attribute of God, and "missionary" is not a title for a special class of workers but an adjective describing the gathered Christian community in its fullness. The implications of the work of Allen, Newbigin, Bosch, and all those they have inspired call the global church to profound self-analysis. Such analysis can be disconcerting, however, because it can soon eclipse the church's authority as an institution in favor of a renewed commitment to the authority of the Holy Spirit and a quest to live as an alternative society faithful to the demands of the reign of God.

In the short time since the publication of that first volume, "missional" has entered the vocabulary of many English-speaking Christians, especially those functioning as ordained ministers, judicatory officials, and seminary professors. As a seminary professor myself, I have followed this sea change with great interest and thanksgiving, but also with a certain wryness. It is hard not to notice that "missionality" has quickly become a fad. There is a rush today to rebaptize everything "missional" without engaging in the systematic change a return to New Testament missiology might demand of us. The two basic claims of the missional movement, that Christendom has failed and was not faithful to the New Testament in any case, have been hard to refute, but their implications have also been difficult to swallow. Christendom may be ending in Europe and North America, but the engine of Constantinian Christianity is still running strong in those with institutional authority. For many it seems easier simply to declare the church's programs "missional" than to engage in any self-reflection or to change any current church practices beyond the level of vocabulary.

But "missional" is far more than a hot new vocabulary word. Like the message of the gospel itself, it calls for *metanoia*, a change of mind. It asks that we stop what we are doing and turn around to see what God is doing. Unfortunately, the steady progress toward the rebirth of a biblical missiology described above has coincided with the decline of mainstream Christianity in the Western world, with the result that few institutional leaders have the patience to stop and turn around; instead, they want the quick answer that will reinvigorate moribund denominations and spread optimism throughout their congregations. As a result, the reemergence of New Testament missiology has in many ways been hijacked by the "maintenance to mission" movement that has swept so much of North American and British Christianity. The notion that churches should not be invested solely in self-preservation but should orient themselves toward the world around them is a fine and important one, but it's also a relatively new idea for most people in the pews. As a result, many "missional" churches are using the word to describe more familiar activities: stepped-up membership recruitment and expanded outreach programs. Again, there is nothing wrong with these emphases per se, but they leave the institutional church very much intact and postpone for a later day reflection on the nature of God and the pattern of God's activity in the world. They also overlook the fact that at the very heart of the sea change represented by the reemergence of missionality is the claim that it is God who is missional, not the church. The church can become missional only by reflecting God's missional nature, not by introducing new programs or sending invitational fliers to potential new members. As theologian Harvie Conn has said, "We are in need of a missiological agenda for theology rather than just a theological agenda for mission."[9]

If mission is not an activity of the church but an attribute of God, what are the implications for preaching? For many of us charged with preaching weekly, our imagination has been constrained by a seminary education rooted in the German university system. Theology was presented to us as a subject to be mastered at beginning, intermediate, and advanced levels. As a result, once we grasp the intellectual distinction between missionality as an activity of the church and missionality as an attribute of God, we may assume that we should either *talk about* the missionality of God, or preach about activities the church should be doing to *reflect* the missionality of God. I hear both options exercised frequently these days as preachers of many denominations become charged up (often quite sincerely) by the opportunity to speak about something other than their two hours of exegesis and the upcoming building campaign. My classes on missional preaching bring clergy back to seminary from all over the country hoping I'll teach them how to "do" what the course promises. It's no pleasure to disappoint them, but we cannot change the habits of seventeen hundred years in a week's seminar or even a full semester's class. If I've learned anything about missional preaching in the past six years, it is that it's hard work, mentally and spiritually. It takes its cue from the announcement of Jesus at the inauguration of his public ministry in the gospel of Mark: "The kingdom of God has come near. Repent and believe in the good news" (Mark 1:15b).

These simple words remind us that the "crisis in preaching" may be due to our long amnesia about the preaching of *krisis*, the judgment of God breaking in to human history. As Canadian theologian Douglas John Hall pointed out, the clergy who preach and the laity who listen are more than familiar with "criticism," pointing out what's wrong with a sermon or a parish or a ministry plan, but neither seems familiar with the *krisis* that "begins with the household of God" (1 Pet. 4:17), a searching examination of the nature and life of a Christian community in the light of God's saving judgment: "[Our] criticism seldom rises above the level of abuse . . . because we have not been able to permit authentic criticism to inform the public, everyday, theological, liturgical and social life of our churches. Great certainty, great commitment, does not fear such criticism." Hall goes on to point out that "when critique of any phenomenon is not permitted openly, we can be sure that it will be engaged in secretly."[10] Although Hall was speaking about the life of the church as a whole, his comment is particularly apt for preaching. Preachers are widely critiqued by their congregations but rarely to their faces, a telling indicator of the lack of true mutuality in the clergy-laity relationship as it exists in most mainline churches. To introduce the notion of judgment in preaching invokes for many the image of the fiery, *judgmental* fundamentalist, condemning listeners for their personal behavior and removing any grounds from which to claim righteousness before God. But what if a renewed preaching of the New Testament understanding of *krisis* could offer preachers and congregations alike the possibility of mutually empowering discernment of the activity of God in their midst?

From Crisis to *Krisis*:
Missional Preaching and the Kingdom of God

In the early twenty-first century, it's not only preaching but the church itself that is facing a crisis. In the United States, the mainline denominations continue to battle apathy and marginalization while a renewed Constantinianism inspires the politically conservative evangelical denominations to make bold demands on elected governments. Their vision of a state-supported and state-enforced Christianity has ample precedent in history and places the evangelicals in the mainstream of a global Christianity fighting for world supremacy with its only remaining rival, Islam. Even as clergy of America's mainline denominations wring their hands when they look to the almost complete attrition of churchgoing in Europe and Great Britain, the clergy of Africa, Asia, and South America have to figure out how to cope with explosive growth while armed conflict threatens many of their communities. Ironically, not a few Christian preachers look to the developing world for models of church growth in the United States and Europe, though the chances of finding genuine parallels remain slim. Even Pope Benedict XVI seemed resigned to a smaller but more effective European Christian community in his first public statements after his election.[11]

The word *krisis* is used forty-seven times in the New Testament, almost never in the sense of our modern word "crisis." While different New Testament authors use it to mean different things, *krisis* ("judgment") unites the gospel and epistle writers around the central proclamation that, in Jesus, God was present in history offering an alternative to human notions of power and destiny and forcing a choice of allegiance. For some New Testament authors, *krisis* happens in an existential encounter with Jesus during his lifetime; for others, it means the final judgment on a world that did not receive "the One sent from the Father."[12] What unites these uses of the word is an urgency to interpret God's intervention in human history and a clear understanding that the world is divided into "then" and "now" by the life, death, and resurrection of Jesus Christ. What further unites the authors who use the word *krisis* to describe God's intervention in history is that they *greet it with joy*.[13] Today a crisis means something we have to fix—fast. For the New Testament it describes a permanent new state of living with one foot in the world where God's reign is the only power to be reckoned with.

Anyone who has been to seminary would find these claims unremarkable, yet these theological assertions about history fail to shape the preaching of most seminary graduates in anything more than an academic way. As Paul Tillich famously said, "We have to . . . overcome the wrong stumbling block in order to bring people face to face with the right stumbling block and enable them to make a genuine decision [for] the Gospel."[14] Sadly, from the most erudite and interesting of preachers to the most hackneyed and unoriginal, the Christian sermon has for a very long time been reduced to the status of an essay on religious ideas or an interesting story with theological significance rather than a life-changing oral event that confronts its hearers with the *krisis* of God's reign breaking into human history and demanding a response of faith and allegiance. Of course, good sermons still change lives, and clergy from many Christian denominations do preach in a way that expects a behavioral response from their listeners, whether baptism or a recommitment to faith in Jesus. But there are no Christian preachers alive today who have not been formed by the habits of what Douglas John Hall called "the Constantinian assumption" that the kingdom of God and the outward and visible institution of the church are identical.[15] As a result, sermons are shaped by the needs of the church rather than by the demands of the kingdom, and therefore cannot avoid becoming consumer products available in a variety of shapes and sizes to be purchased by the religious listener/shopper. Isn't that why books on preaching proliferate like cookbooks? There is always the hope that the offering can be improved and generate more customers for the franchise, perhaps even resulting in a bonus or promotion for the manager.

Unfortunately, Jesus did not send the Twelve or the Seventy to offer sermons that people would enjoy or find meaningful. "He sent them out to proclaim the kingdom of God and to heal" (Luke 9:2).

> "Whenever you enter a town and its people welcome you, eat what is set before you; cure the sick who are there, and say to them, 'The kingdom of God has come near to you.' But whenever you enter a town and they do not welcome you, go out into the streets and say 'Even the dust of your town that clings to our feet, we wipe off in protest against you. Yet know this: the kingdom of God has come near.'"
>
> Luke 10:8-11

Krisis indeed! The verb translated "proclaim" by the New Revised Standard Version of the Bible was translated "preach" by the King James Version. So the first "sent ones" (*apostelmenoi*, apostles) are sent to preach the kingdom of God and to heal, and their listeners are asked to make a life-determining choice about their message—a tall order for the typical preacher of the early twenty-first century who is charged with attracting and holding members to an institution that depends on their voluntary donations to survive.

"Let the dead bury their own dead; but as for you, go and proclaim the kingdom of God" (Luke 9:60). I am entirely sympathetic to the numerous fine and earnest preachers in the pulpits of North American churches today, many of whom are executing with their whole hearts and minds excellent versions of the sermon models they were taught to create in seminary. But when a group of clergy gathers for a workshop on missional preaching and virtually no one has any content for "the kingdom of God" other than church membership now or heaven later, we do indeed have a crisis. We don't need to improve our product; we need to change our minds about it.

CHAPTER 2

The Quick Fix Is No Longer an Option

For seven years in the 1990s I was pastor of a small Episcopal parish in the western suburbs of Chicago. Membership had declined steadily over the previous twenty years until only a remnant of the original congregation was still in place upon my arrival, but that remnant was both faithful and energized. The physical plant was meticulously maintained, and the small congregation was genuinely welcoming. The congregation had mourned the loss of many members over the years, but the only vision for the future was one of hanging on: "maintenance" with an edge of desperation.

During the nineties the possibility of orienting congregations away from "maintenance" toward "mission" became widely known and adopted[1] by the leaders of mainline denominations and the burgeoning roster of congregational development consultants. This change of vocabulary represented the trickle-down effect of the work of Allen, Newbigin, and Bosch described in the previous chapter, packaged for easy consumption, and it came at a time when the church-growth movement was looking for marketable approaches for churches hemorrhaging members. This pattern of thinking came to me primarily through the work of Howard Hanchey, at that time professor of pastoral theology at Virginia Theological Seminary, and I recommended that the members of the parish council each read his short book *From Survival to Celebration*.[2] A key concept of Hanchey's work, and of all the works of this genre, is that "mission" should no longer be considered one activity of the church among many, but the reason for which the church exists. Thus, "outreach committees" or "mission boards" would be discontinued in favor of thinking of the whole parish as "mission-oriented," the entire church budget would be viewed as the servant of God's mission, and so on. I liked Hanchey's book because it had such concrete suggestions for helping with the sea change these ideas represented.

One of Hanchey's ideas that the parish council decided to implement right away was the reordering of its meetings to *begin* with the future and *end* with the past.[3] In other words, we began to use the time at the beginning of the meeting when we had the most energy to talk about new visions and emerging ministries within the congregation, while saving reports about buildings and grounds and the budget for the end of the meeting. Although this information might be important, it was about the past, and to give it pride of place made the meetings a constant rehash of what had already taken place. This simple change proved revolutionary for my small community's board meetings, and we came to look forward to our monthly gatherings instead of dreading them. Rather than spending half an hour on the various models of water heaters we could buy to replace the old one, we began to ask what God was doing in our midst and in our surrounding community. This reorientation also meant that Sunday announcements and written and electronic communications were constantly about the future instead of the past. But we didn't simply become a forward-looking organization. Encouraging the congregation's leadership to think in a systematic and habitual way about God's work in our midst and in the world shaped these individuals as practical theologians who looked for the places their community could participate in God's abundant life rather than simply planning predetermined activities. As this mindset became widespread, even the outer ring of attenders became aware that the parish was excited about the way God's life was being welcomed on many fronts.

The real transformation of this parish from "maintenance" to "mission" took a number of years. Eventually the members of longest standing were able to let go of the idea that their inadequate stewardship had been responsible for the loss of so many parishioners. They had thought they needed to improve their product, to develop a program no other local church offered to entice and retain new members. In fact, what they had was quite enough: the reign of God lived out in a weekly experience of vital worship and daily works of mercy offered unassumingly by people of deep faith and self-deprecating humor. It took my new set of eyes coming from the outside to see their wealth at a time when they felt very poor and, indeed, had been told to expect closure by the diocese. We formed a "missional partnership" without ever using the words.

So while "maintenance to mission" was becoming all the rage in seminary education and denominational conferences, I was participating in it directly in a congregational setting. What soon became obvious was that my preaching could not continue unchanged if the community I was preaching to was reorienting itself toward the mission of God in the world. My preaching was well received by the congregation, even popular. I didn't need to be a better preacher; I needed to have a different image for what I was doing, and I needed to approach the Scriptures through a different lens. I needed to become a missional preacher reading the Bible as a missional document. But the professors who had prepared me to preach, while excellent, had never heard the word "missional" and probably would not have approved of it if they had. Priority had been given to careful exegesis of the Scriptures and the systematic development of a homiletical message in a text that placed a high value on the right word in the right place. The preaching I was taught was rooted in the timeless life of the Scriptures, not the contingent life of congregations. Although no one would have said so at the time, my seminary education had prepared me for maintenance, not mission, and the self-image it offered me as preacher was something between a university professor and a salesman: I had to *inform* and *persuade*.

I've Been to Seminary (And You Haven't): Information

When I was a child in the 1960s, my public elementary school's Christmas pageant was all about the birth of Jesus (and Santa and snowmen, of course). It was the last gasp of an unreflective synthesis of Christianity and American public life, something many churches are trying to hang onto or revive today: prayer at football games and baccalaureate services led by clergy. While the divorce of church and state is by no means complete, the trial separation has been pretty effective. Compared to Americans of the eighteenth and nineteenth centuries, we move in a cultural milieu largely devoid of biblical content. The courts have ruled that it is the business of religious institutions and families to teach the content of religious belief systems, and some denominations have been better at picking up the slack than others. Roman Catholics, Missouri Synod Lutherans, and Mormons offer vigorous programs outside the traditional Sunday hours for educating children and teens, but adult education in mainline churches is largely an elective, and most churchgoers feel they've put in their time just attending the worship service. It's too hard to schedule the day if you need to come early or stay late for a seminar or Bible class. So the principal opportunity for communicating the content of the Christian faith is largely restricted to the Sunday sermon. The burden this places on the preacher is enormous: here's your chance to teach the whole Christian faith in brief intervals spread over fifty-two Sundays. Few, if any, clergy were given a model to do this kind of teaching, however. The only model most have to draw on is the seminary classroom.

While pedagogy in theological education is a hot topic in the early twenty-first century, it was not when most preachers today were getting their seminary educations. Most were taught as though they were graduate students in religion, with a lecture-based model that came naturally to their faculty, most of whom earned their Ph.D.s in a program of biblical or theological studies that assumed a background in the humanities. (Courses in "practical theology" and the practice of ministry, including preaching, are routinely listed last in seminary catalogues, and these "lesser" courses are often taught by practitioners lacking a Ph.D.) Ironically, teachers of preschool and elementary-age children are required to have extensive training and certification before they can be let loose on their charges, but graduate school (including seminary) can be taught by anyone with the appropriate higher degree. The ability to teach well is valued but not a prerequisite, since there is no systematic approach to teaching the teachers of graduate students.

If the preacher you listen to Sunday after Sunday was lectured to for three years while getting her master of divinity degree, the lecture will be the logical model for her to build on. After all, she quickly realizes how much teaching she'll need to do if her sermons are to make full sense to her congregation. If the lectures she heard in seminary were riveting and inspiring, this approach may produce a good result for the listening congregation, assuming she has abilities similar to those of her best professors. If she doesn't, or if the lectures she heard bored her to tears, she may choose to avoid overt instruction during the sermon and shoot for "religious meaning." For instance, rather than conveying information on the background of the Ten Commandments and their relation to other ancient systems of laws, she may tell a story illustrating the value of having a shared code of conduct in a diverse society. Such an approach can certainly be justified in a post-Christendom world in which religious language is little understood and religion itself can become a polarizing force. Offer your listeners an idea they can use in their daily lives, the reasoning goes, and they'll become more interested in the tradition and want to learn more. But there are pitfalls to this indirect approach in an era when religious knowledge is at an all-time low. One doctoral student of mine reports preaching a sermon on a passage from Luke's Gospel and being asked at the door by an educated, professional parishioner who had very much enjoyed the sermon: "Is Luke the name of your husband?"[4]

Other clergy, particularly in megachurches, have capitalized on the hunger for religious instruction and have explicitly embraced the lecture format in their preaching, often enhancing its presentation with PowerPoint projections that incorporate music or video clips or live drama that incarnates the day's message. There is much to be said for the effectiveness of this approach, though supersizing a traditional ecclesiology and making it more accessible is no guarantee of missionality. And clergy who do not serve megachurches but choose the self-identity of teacher in the pulpit can end up resembling nothing so much as docents, the volunteers at art galleries and historic sites who have boned up on the specific offerings of their venues and share their knowledge with precision and grace. Docents, however, get to speak to audiences that have chosen to visit the gallery or landmark out of interest in it; the weekly congregation cannot be said to have been motivated by the same spontaneity. People come for a whole variety of reasons, from habit to a search for community to help with raising their children; and the preacher must somehow find a way to connect with their initial motivations and convert those impulses to ongoing membership commitments (another burden not placed on docents—only on their development offices). The preacher-as-docent needs not only to inform the congregation about a biblical or theological subject, but then to persuade listeners that it has something to do with the lives they left outside the church door.

The "So What?" Factor: Persuasion

As if the information gap between clergy and laity in mainline denominations were not a significant enough problem for the weekly challenge of preaching, the fact that life can go on without one's knowing whether Isaiah 35 is truly a misplaced portion of Deutero-Isaiah increases the challenges the sermon writer faces. Once she has informed the congregants about the things they never knew about God or the Bible, how does she persuade her listeners to care about this information? As a teacher of preaching, I find this one of the hardest obstacles to surmount with my students. For three years, their entire world is saturated with churchspeak, and their ears are no longer attuned to the specialized nature of their language. I point out that their preaching classes may be the last time anyone like me will reflect the out-of-touchness of their messages to them; most congregations are far too polite to tell a preacher that they had no idea what he was talking about. Unfortunately, many seminarians enter the parish committed to persuading congregations that what their seminary encouraged them to consider interesting and important *should be* of interest and importance to their non-seminary-trained listeners. Most preachers have no way of getting genuine feedback on what people are actually hearing in their sermons or what the sermons mean to them, and many clergy react defensively to anything but praise at the door on Sunday. Those who are self-aware enough to recognize the hunger behind the polite smiles and kind words at coffee hour may begin to orient themselves toward their audience's concerns. Instead of preaching about what seminary taught them to care about, they may begin to ask what their *parishioners* care about and compose their sermons accordingly. Such sensitivity to the captive audience of a congregation is to be commended, and preachers who do this with any kind of flair become immensely popular. But it does not take much reflection to see that this approach can become a self-referential loop, a recipe for church maintenance made appealing.

The New Testament portrays large crowds following Jesus to hear his words. It is unclear exactly how much education Jesus might have had; some scholars today believe he may have been able to read Hebrew and speak common Greek, while others believe that given his social milieu he could only have been illiterate. What is clear is that Jesus was not regarded as a "teacher of the Law" in the sense of being a scholar allied with the religious establishment, one "authorized" to teach the people of Israel. In contemporary terms, he was not seminary-educated. Yet audiences comprising the entire spectrum of ancient society are portrayed as finding life-changing value in his words. Of course, the gospels are biased documents, crafted to convey a persuasive picture of Jesus for believer and nonbeliever alike. Nonetheless, it is notable that the authors of the gospels do not show Jesus relaying information in language that requires a special education to understand, and he seems never to have to persuade his listeners that what he is saying is important for their lives. They may reject his message or embrace it, but educated and uneducated alike seem to understand it. Naturally, there has been a lot of water under the bridge in two thousand years, and preachers today are speaking in the context of a long-established religious tradition unknown to Jesus. But the *life-changing* quality of the remembered words of Jesus is surely worth considering by people who continue to speak in his name and believe that their speech is a part of God's salvation. That means that if we were taught to preach like docents, professors, or salespeople, we may have to rethink what we're getting up to do when we enter the pulpit on Sunday morning, because none of these models can live up to the model Jesus gave his first preachers.

Rethinking Ourselves as Preachers

The transformation of my own identity as a preacher began with noticing the inadequacy of my image of the preacher. I had consumed my seminary education voraciously and had gone on reading and teaching in various venues ever since: I had a lot to share! But in the mid-1990s I began to ask whether making the Christian tradition—its ideas about God, its sacred texts, its liturgical practices—accessible and user-friendly to my listeners was what I really needed to be doing. An incident that occurred in worship one morning made me see my preaching ministry in an entirely new and not wholly favorable light.

We had the Montessori-based Catechesis of the Good Shepherd as our program for children in that parish, and the children's classroom, called an atrium, had child-sized copies of the key furniture of our church: altar, font, lectern, etc. One day a smaller copy of the tabernacle (a sort of wall safe for the reservation of consecrated bread and wine) was added to their room and presented to the children. At the end of worship that day, I brought them to the front of the church to see the tabernacle from which theirs had been copied. "What do you see that is like something you saw in the atrium today?" I asked. The children all pointed at the tabernacle on the wall behind the altar. "And what is that called?" "The tabernacle!" they all said together. "Can someone show us what the tabernacle is used for?" A five-year old girl walked behind the altar, opened the tabernacle, and took the silver bread box from within. She held it up to the congregation and said, "This is the ciborium. It holds the bread of Jesus." The congregation beamed as the little girl took the ciborium back to its home and closed the door again. Many later remarked on how "cute" her demonstration was, but the fact was that few members of the congregation could have accurately named the box on the wall behind the altar, much less the vessel kept inside. But the culture of the church often makes adults feel uncomfortable asking basic questions about things they don't understand but feel they should. So the child's demonstration became a safe way for adults to learn.

What was a source of wonder and discovery for a five-year-old, however, became mere information for most of the congregation. Being better informed about the name of the ornate silver vessel inside the elaborately carved wooden box made them feel more confident about the practices of their religion, but it had not necessarily revealed something essential about God to them. When the items were first presented to them in their dedicated space, the children in the atrium had had a chance to wonder aloud about the tabernacle and the ciborium and what it all meant about God and God's place in their lives. When would the congregation have such an opportunity?

It was then that I began to wonder whether my preaching was like the little girl's demonstration of the ciborium without the ensuing reflection and engagement. Was I, in effect, holding up the texts of the Bible week by week to the congregation and simply giving my listeners information about those texts, even if that information was more subtle and complex than the five-year-old's identification of the ciborium? Was I speaking as the seminary-trained "expert" to the "uneducated" laity? Certainly this was no part of my conscious understanding of what I was doing, but I began to question the ways my own education and the ordination process itself had formed me in such a model despite my best intentions.

North American culture has a love/hate relationship with experts. It has become *de rigueur* for hired presenters to disown the role of "expert" in favor of a title like "facilitator," but if the content is thin, the "facilitators" will likely hear about it and not get a second invitation. On the other hand, our television news programs cannot get through a major story without inviting an expert to comment on unfolding events. In the context of the church, clergy are expected to *be* experts but not *act like* experts. In a maintenance model, such a role is manageable, since the clergy are paid a salary to use their education to lead all aspects of the community and to deliver an attractive product on Sundays that people will want to support with their monetary offerings. Being

an expert carries a great deal of authority in a maintenance context, but the economic side of the transaction provides a check and
balance on that authority. Because the expertise is being paid for,
the congregation can admonish or fire the ordained leader who
cannot preach, lead worship, or provide effective pastoral care. As
long as those products are being delivered satisfactorily, however,
the clergyperson who has not offended still carries a great deal of
authority.

For ordained leaders striving to move a congregation from
maintenance to mission, that authority can be a burden. Although
the language of ministry has changed radically since the Second
World War with the reemergence of baptism as the fundamental
icon of the Christian life, most of the baptized continue to look
outside themselves for the interpretation of Scripture and the theological meaning of life. Denominational white papers and worship
resources may emphasize the ministry of the whole people of God,
but the continued pattern of raising up a caste of professional
clergy, and educating and paying them, ultimately diminishes the
vast amount of lay ministry that is not raised up or compensated.
The fact is, being specially trained and being paid a living wage
both confer *agency*—the power to act—on individuals. Inversely,
having little education and serving as a volunteer do not offer the
same conviction of agency, even when it is "officially" conferred
from the pulpit or service leaflet. It has become a commonplace to
ask what congregation members might do *as* the church (outside
of worship) rather than *for* the church (assisting in worship and
maintaining the facilities). But this cultural shift still exists more
dramatically on the pages of prayer books and denominational
manifestos than it does in society at large, where churches are still
largely viewed as voluntaristic organizations, like garden clubs
and the Shriners, or sites for self-improvement, like libraries and
health clubs. The typical churchgoer in North America may be
complimented to know that he or she has a ministry to be claimed
and exercised in the world, but most cannot get past a lifetime of
formation that said clergy bear the lion's share of responsibility
for anything properly called ministry. So the icon of the clergy
leader is both a threat and an opportunity for missional preaching:
a threat, because the clergy leader has been trained and hired to

maintain and grow an institution whose focus is self-perpetuation; an opportunity, because if the church is going to live into a new ecclesiology, the pulpit will be one of the most powerful tools to effect that change.

CHAPTER 3

The Kingdom of God and Healing: The New Testament Model

So if missional preaching is not a new and improved version of preaching for maintenance, what is it? One of the consistent hallmarks of missional theology is turning to the Bible for its defining paradigms, paying special attention to the New Testament. Even as I had begun to form ideas about what missional preaching *wasn't,* I didn't have a clear idea about what it actually might look and sound like. So my first impulse when I began to teach classes on the subject of missional preaching was to see whether such a thing is described anywhere in the gospels. The answer, alluded to in the first chapter of this book, was revelatory.

We get our word "mission" from the Latin verb "to send": *mitto, mittere, misi, missum.*[1] The word comes to us through Latin because Latin superseded Greek as the language of the church. The verb "to send" in New Testament Greek is *apostellein.* From these sources, we get two common English words, "missionary" and "apostle." The verb "to preach" in Greek is *keryssein,* from *keryx,* or "herald." *Keryssein* tends to get translated as "proclaim" in the gospels (John the Baptist "proclaiming" in the wilderness," Luke 3:3-4), and "preach" in the rest of the New Testament, where it used to describe the work of the first apostles ("sent ones") in proclaiming the good news *about* Jesus rather than the good news proclaimed *by* Jesus.[2] Both words, *apostellein* and *keryssein,* are common throughout the New Testament. What I wanted to know was whether they were ever used jointly: is anyone ever "sent" "to preach" in the New Testament? Is there "missional preaching" in Scripture? I found that the words were indeed used together, in a passage that has since become foundational to my thinking about missional preaching.

> Then Jesus called the twelve together and gave them power and authority over all demons and to cure diseases, and he *sent* [*apostellein*] them out to *proclaim* [*keryssein*] the *kingdom of God* and to *heal*. He said to them, "Take nothing for your journey, no staff, nor bag, nor bread, nor money—not even an extra tunic. Whatever house you enter, stay there, and leave from there. Wherever they do not welcome you, as you are leaving that town shake the dust off your feet as a testimony against them." They departed and went through the villages, bringing the good news and curing diseases everywhere.
>
> Now Herod the ruler heard about all that had taken place, and he was perplexed, because it was said by some that John had been raised from the dead, by some that Elijah had appeared, and by others that one of the ancient prophets had arisen. Herod said, "John I beheaded; but who is this about whom I hear such things?" And he tried to see him.
>
> On their return the *apostles* [those "sent" by Jesus] told Jesus all they had done. He took them with him and withdrew privately to a city called Bethsaida. When the crowds found out about it, they followed him; and he welcomed them, and *spoke to them about the kingdom of God*, and *healed* those who needed to be cured.
>
> Luke 9:1-11, emphases added

The words are linked again in the parallel passages of Mark 3:14 and Matthew 10:5-7, but the Lukan example of missional preaching proved the richest of the three and provided me with the model that the rest of this book will flesh out. Here are the highlights of what I noticed in Luke's account:

- Missional preachers are sent by Jesus, not by an institution.
- Missional preachers are empowered by Jesus specifically for their work of proclamation.

- Missional preachers proclaim the kingdom of God.
- The proclamation of the kingdom of God is accompanied by healing.
- The people who hear missional preaching experience it as a "crisis" (*krisis*): a moment of free decision for or against the kingdom of God.
- Missional preachers travel light.
- Jesus does what he sends his preachers to do: he speaks about the kingdom of God and heals.
- Missional preaching brings the preachers to the attention of the secular government.

Let's look at each of these characteristics of missional preaching in turn.

Missional Preachers Are Sent by Jesus

The notion that missional preachers are sent by Jesus may seem too obvious to bear comment, but it's an essential starting point. Naturally, there was no organized church to send preachers during the period depicted by the gospels, and, by the era of their composition, the newly forming church was indeed sending preachers out into the world. However, it is not clear that the two groups of preachers—those in Jesus's day and those subsequent to it—had the same agenda. The preachers described in the gospels as sent by Jesus preach the kingdom of God and its arrival among the listeners; those sent by the church in subsequent generations preach Christ, and him crucified, and frequently invite baptism or church membership as a response. Just as we create nativity scenes that unite and harmonize the birth narratives of Luke and Matthew, placing shepherds and magi in a single Italianate grotto, Christians from the first to the twenty-first century tend to assume that the kingdom and Jesus are all part of the same message. Certainly, a case can be made for their unity, but too little attention has been given to the content of the earliest missional preaching portrayed in the Scriptures. The Lukan Jesus "came to bring fire to the earth" (Luke 12:49), and he is impatient to see it kindled. He has come to announce the direct reign of God on earth, not in the person of a messianic king but in the formation of communities of resistance to the widespread dehumanization inflicted by the combined oppression of Rome and the house of Herod. (More about this in chapter 4.) When he sends preachers, their commission is to repeat his proclamation and carry on his work: the kingdom of God is among you to be lived out now; it's not pie in the sky by and by.

Many men and women who go off to seminary do so with a profound awareness of being "sent" there: by an inner conviction, by their local church communities, by their family and friends, by God, or by all of these. Like the Lukan Jesus, they often describe an eagerness to share the flame of passion they feel within themselves with the wider world. Many, if not most, report losing this conviction during their time in seminary. It might be the shock of learning a historical-critical approach to Scripture, or feeling overwhelmed by the often-arcane language of professional theologians, or struggling to maintain a sense of identity during the ordination process. Whatever the cause, most seminarians come to realize that they are graduate students with the attendant cynicism that plagues that limbo-like existence, and many long to be released back into the "real world" of the church they now remember nostalgically. Unfortunately, the liminal experience of seminary means that the church they remember fondly is no longer accessible to them when seminary is over, since their education and the privileges of ordination mandate a new relationship to the community of believers that sent them off years earlier.

When I ask my doctoral students, practicing clergy many years out of seminary, what the transition from seminary into professional ministry was like for them, most report a process of being trained and hired similar to that of other jobs, even in those denominations that use the language and practice of "sending" clergy to ministry appointments. Their self-images after years of preaching form a list like this:

Social activist
Politician
Entertainer
Clown

Social worker
Mentor
Poet
Shepherd
Midwife
Essayist
Cheerleader
Enabler
Storyteller
Lifeguard
Salesperson
Motivational speaker
Nag
Parent

The images on this list, compiled from the input of numerous clergy over several years, were not intended by those who offered them as cynical complaints but as honest descriptions of what these men and women feel as they exercise their pulpit ministry. Some of these images are powerful and helpful, but none reveals that sense of being "sent by Jesus" described by the gospel author.[3] Yet practicing clergy unanimously feel enlivened and encouraged by the possibility of reclaiming the conviction of "sentness" that made them choose their professional path in life. It almost seems as though being "sent by the church" has become drained of meaning for many clergy, aware as they are that the expectations of the sending church primarily involve numerical and financial growth. The notion of being "sent by Jesus" awakens a different sense of what the agenda for preaching might be.

Missional Preachers Are Empowered by Jesus

If the preachers sent by Jesus were merely going to present inspirational messages to help people think better thoughts and improve their lives, they wouldn't need any special empowerment. The fact that they are given power to "cure all diseases" as well as "authority over all demons" before they set out indicates that

their involvement with their listeners is going to be far more challenging than simply presenting helpful ideas about God and the
soul. Since the Enlightenment, scholars and preachers have tended
to read these stories of healing power with the assumption that
people in the first century were naive about the body and health.
Such an assumption leads us to think of Jesus's commissioning of
the apostles as the training of a medical team. Many Bible commentaries and seminary Scripture classes approach the healings of
the New Testament as rooted in ignorance, arguing that what the
New Testament calls "demonic possession" would be diagnosed
today as epilepsy or some other medical condition. The explosion
of information about the historical Jesus and his period that has
become widely available in the past twenty-five years has forced
us to reconceive such assumptions, however. While there is no
consensus about just what Jesus was training his followers to be
and do, there can be little doubt that it involved a controversial
challenge to the status quo, one guaranteed to stir up a strong response. Today we have considerably more information about the
world Jesus lived in. That information makes it possible to realize
that what gets healed by Jesus and by the preachers he sends are
not simply diseases and mental conditions undiagnosable by the
medical profession of the time. Rather, they may be seen more
truly as symptoms of the out-of-whackness of life under Herod
and Rome manifesting itself as disease and demonic possession.
In their book *The Message and the Kingdom*, scholars of religion
Richard Horsley and Neil Silberman write:

> Early Christianity was . . . a down-to-earth response to an op
> pressive ideology of earthly power that had recently swept across
> continents, disrupted economies, and overturned ancient tradi
> tions. [Jesus] directly addressed the painful specifics of peasant
> life under the rule of Herod Antipas, offering his listeners far
> more than just generalized promises or threats. In Jesus's pres
> ence or under his influence, people who had been previously par
> alyzed or crippled by forces beyond their control began to piece
> their lives back together, for he offered them both a new feeling
> of community and a new personal confidence.[4]

Such a framework of interpretation makes far greater sense of Jesus's eventual execution at the hands of the occupying government. To proclaim the direct rule of God to a people suffering the effects of the rule of Herod or Rome would certainly be to take one's life in one's hands; hence the need to travel light and have special powers of speech and touch and a sense of authority to challenge the forces that corrupt and degrade human society. When we look through the front section of our newspapers today, we don't have to look far to see similar forces of corruption and degradation. What if our preaching challenged these forces? Is the power of Jesus still available to us for such a proclamation? Would it cost us as much as it cost him?

Missional Preachers Proclaim the Kingdom of God

New information about the first century of the Christian era is helping us to realize that the proclamation of the kingdom of God may have sounded quite different to the ears of Jesus's first listeners from the way it sounds to our own, both more specific and more revolutionary. Most of us have heard our fair share of sermons about how the people of Jesus's day were anticipating a military-political messiah, requiring Jesus to shatter common expectations and realign them by teaching about a kingdom at once more universal and more spiritual. Now historical Jesus scholarship is calling our assumptions along these lines into question:

> Jesus suggested that God was establishing His Kingdom by creating an alternative society. Villagers who could have cooperated in their own liberation were at each others' throats. Jesus's healings and teachings must be therefore seen in this context, not as abstract spiritual truths spoken between stunning miracles but as a program of community action and practical resistance to a system that efficiently transformed close-knit villages into badly fragmented communities of alienated, frightened individuals. Such cooperation and mutual assistance were what the age-old covenantal tradition had fostered and articulated, and we must

see these teachings as a practical response to the contemporary political and economic situation of the people of Galilee under Herodian rule. The mission of Jesus's disciples was an ambitious yet down-to-earth attempt to overturn the accepted order through a revolution in the people's behavior; it was not a program of purely spiritual conversion.[5]

In the following chapter, we'll look at how the kingdom of God has become a concept very different in our thoughts and prayers from what the New Testament seems to be speaking of. For now, it is enough to note that the kingdom of God—God's reign on earth, here and now—is the sole content assigned to the "sent preachers" of Luke 9. The directive apparently sums up all of Jesus's public ministry since its inauguration at Capernaum (Luke 4). We might even say that the announcement of God's direct reign weaves together all of Luke's carefully composed narrative to that point. The preparatory annunciations, the divine choice to ignore human systems of power and to bring the poor, the old, and the disenfranchised into God's inner circle (pushing aside those currently claiming to rule from that place of privilege), and radical new ideas about wealth and blessing, poverty, and disfavor—these are all evidence of a new form of government on the earth. There can be little doubt from the first eight chapters of Luke's Gospel that the kingdom of God which the first missional preachers are sent to proclaim has distinct political and economic implications.

The Proclamation of the Kingdom of God Is Accompanied by Healing

As a demonstration of the power of God, Moses turned his staff into a serpent and called down all manner of plagues upon the oppressive government of the Egyptians (Exod. 7-12). To challenge the government of Rome and its collaborators, however, the first missional preachers are told to demonstrate God's power through healing. If Luke's narrative up to this point is any indication of his understanding of that word, then healing is to be extended across racial, ethnic, and socioeconomic lines, and it represents a further proclamation of the kingdom of God rather than a personal favor to the sufferer. Thus far in Luke's narrative, Jesus has healed (or exorcised) Jews and Gentiles, city dwellers and farm laborers, and has empowered free people and slaves, men and women deemed outcast by their peers, even children. He has set a high bar and cast a very wide net for his "sent ones" to imitate and has extended the reach of his stated mission to offer the jubilee, "the year of the Lord's favor" (Luke 4:19) to an audience much broader than than Israel alone. John Dominic Crossan sums up the revolutionary aspects of this program of healing:

> Excessive taxation could leave poor people physically malnourished or hysterically disabled. But since the religiopolitical ascendancy could not blame excessive taxation, it blamed sick people themselves by claiming that their sins had led to their illnesses. And the cure for sinful sickness was, ultimately, in the Temple. And that meant more fees, in a perfect circle of victimization. When, therefore . . . Jesus with a magical touch cured people of their sicknesses, [he] implicitly declared their sins forgiven or nonexistent. [He] challenged not the medical monopoly of the doctors but the religious monopoly of the priests. All of this was religiopolitically subversive.[6]

Spiritual healing is enjoying a renaissance at the start of the twenty-first century, even coming to the attention of health-insurance companies that may sponsor training programs for hospital chaplains on the basis of studies showing that people who are prayed for go home more quickly. So when we consider the link between preaching the kingdom of God and healing, we may draw on our associations with the relationship between Christian faith and the medical profession today. As we learn more about Jesus's original context, however, we begin to realize that the healing he enjoins his followers to offer is part and parcel of a larger missional plan for proclaiming the kingdom of God present on earth. In many ways clergy and other pastoral caregivers have become the servants of the "real" healers today—physicians and nurses—offering a kind of added value to the procedure, operation, or course of medication that will generally be credited with improving or saving the patient's life. Without diminishing the vital work of health-care professionals in any way, we can ask whether there are not larger problems in need of healing in our world today—problems of access and opportunity, fair wages and adequate education. Physical suffering can be the symptom of these larger problems, as any visit to an emergency room reveals. Elected officials, social workers, and community organizers each contribute their best to solutions, but their audiences are circumscribed. Preachers have a unique opportunity to reach a cross-section of listeners with a vision of God's reign lived out in particular ways in our neighborhoods and cities. Physicians are quick to say when their own expertise has reached its limits; have preachers even tested theirs?

The People Who Hear Missional Preaching Experience It as a "Crisis"

The Lukan Jesus is not above threatening the audiences his "sent ones" will encounter. As a result, our attention tends to gravitate toward the unfortunate towns whose dust will be shaken off of the apostles' feet. After all, a subsequent passage warns the towns of Chorazin and Bethsaida that "at the judgment it will more tolerable for Tyre and Sidon than for you" (Luke 10:14). But if we focus on a potential punishment, we overlook a real difference between the expectations held by the first missional preachers and some common expectations preachers share today. Jesus does not direct the sent ones to try to persuade anyone of the value of their message. The fact that he gives instructions for what to do if the apostolic preaching is received and what to do if it is not received indicates that Jesus can imagine listeners' choosing to reject the message of the kingdom. No doubt this perspective determines his choice to tell the sent ones to *proclaim* rather than to inform, to *demonstrate* the reign of God rather than simply to talk about it, and to accompany that demonstration with acts of healing that allow listeners to receive and participate in the kingdom that has been proclaimed to them. If we assume, in light of later triumphalist Christian theology, that those who reject the message of the apostles are condemned by God, the option to decline the offer may not seem a particularly attractive feature of this first missional preaching. If we choose to believe that Jesus wills the salvation of every human being, we may be perplexed that he does not give the sent ones better training in the arts of persuasion. But recognizing that the decision for or against the kingdom is a free one and *out of the hands* of the preacher has proved a liberating message for beginning and seasoned preachers alike. It means that the preaching task ceases to be about finding ways to gain acceptance of the message. Now it becomes a search for the clearest way to make the proclamation, and then to release it.

Missional Preachers Travel Light

The somewhat perplexing injunction of Jesus to "take nothing for your journey" is helpfully explained by New Testament scholar John Dominic Crossan in his discussion of *commensality*—meal-sharing—as a practice of the kingdom of God: "The missionaries do not carry a bag because they do not beg for alms or food or clothing or anything else. They share a miracle and a Kingdom, and they receive in return a table and a house."[7] While this arrangement may sound distinctly like a modern-day parsonage allowance, there is a mutual accountability in the mission of Jesus's first sent preachers which is quite different from the horse-trading negotiations that lead to a compensation package. The preachers in Luke 9 have an important gift to give, but it is a gift that will go on giving long after they have departed for other audiences. They are not using their message to support themselves for life; they simply need food, clothing, and shelter for the duration of their message-sharing mission. The larger question raised by this passage—whether the practice of having full-time professional clergy has a basis in the New Testament—is beyond the scope of this book. For the purposes of developing a model of missional preaching, it is enough to note that missional preachers travel light because they have an expectation that they are not alone in this business of proclamation; their listeners will become their colleagues and coworkers. The preachers are convicted of the life-changing value of their message and need only embody it to fulfill

their mandate: they don't need a library of commentaries to back
them up. This aspect of the New Testament paradigm has proven
similarly enlivening for the students in my classes, because in it
they discover a reconnection to the feelings of mutuality they had
in the church communities that sent them off to seminary. Freed of
the burden of "the cure of souls," they eagerly anticipate a model
of preaching in which the message's effectiveness will be demonstrated by the increasing evidence of the practices of the kingdom
in the communities where they preach and not by compliments at
the front door on Sunday morning.

Jesus Does What He Sends His Preachers to Do

The idea that our preaching is modeled on that of Jesus himself
is different from what most preachers today believe they are doing. Instead of serving as apprentices to Jesus's work of living the
kingdom and then apprenticing others to share that life, they point
back to Jesus as the only one who actually "does the work" of
the kingdom. As we continue to unpack this Lukan paradigm,
it is striking that the author portrays Jesus as sharing the work
he sends his apostles to do, rather than supplanting it. In Luke's
narrative we glimpse an apprenticeship model of training, one in
which the master and the pupils are engaged in identical work,
rather than a hired-servant model in which the servants remain
perpetually dependent on the orders of the master. This way of
thinking about preaching has proven more difficult for students in
my classes who are accustomed to thinking of the work of Jesus
and their own work as being quite distinct. As we will see later on,
this aspect of mutuality has implications for how preachers relate
to their listeners as well as how they relate to Jesus.

Missional Preaching Brings the Preachers to the
Attention of the Secular Government

The older clergy who mentored me as a newly ordained person
twenty-five years ago remembered a time when it was common
practice to see passages from their Sunday sermons quoted in the

newspapers on Monday morning. In the 1940s and 1950s, the place of Christianity in American society was comfortably secure, and sermon excerpts were viewed as no more controversial or intrusive than "Dear Abby." However, this kind of attention is fundamentally different from Luke's reference to Herod's nervous curiosity about Jesus. A more fitting modern parallel might be the kind of attention that was given to preachers during the Civil Rights movement of the 1960s, when the preaching of many prominent black leaders frequently caused a nervous federal government to eavesdrop on other aspects of their lives. In recent decades, the rise in political involvement by evangelical Christians has forged a new kind of relationship between preaching and politics. What is noteworthy about the Lukan paradigm in this respect is that the missional preachers are not setting out to comment on political conditions; only their proclamation that God has done an end run around all forms of human power puts them on the secular government's screen. Just as twenty-first century preachers would do well to reconsider the broader implications of the kingdom's power to heal, so they might also revisit a school of thought that has become known somewhat patronizingly as "the Social Gospel." Already contextualized by church historians as a "movement" within nineteenth- and twentieth-century Christian thought, the Social Gospel has no clear successor today except a wholesale return to private piety. Unless missional preachers believe firmly that God and Jesus are perfectly content with the state of the world, it's hard to see how they can accept a call to be "sent" and yet not expect some sort of change to result. Jesus's preaching and that of his sent ones brought the combined wrath of politics and religion down upon them. How much comfort are we willing to sacrifice for the sake of our preaching?

Truly a Paradigm?

The reader who has followed me this far may well have some questions. Is this book simply an argument for preaching the historical Jesus rather than the Christ of faith, and thus for a style of preaching limited to the most liberal end of mainstream Christianity? What about the so-called Great Commission of Matthew 28?

Isn't that an equally appropriate scriptural paradigm for missional preaching? These are the aspects of missional preaching that the rest of this book will unpack and explore.

CHAPTER 4

Reimagining the Kingdom of God

When I ask groups of preachers, whether seminarians, doctoral students, or practicing clergy, if they ever preach about the kingdom of God, very few say that they do. Pressed to supply some content for the phrase, preachers typically offer one of two primary references: life after death or the visible, institutional church and its activities. The first idea of the kingdom of God shows up at funerals and in sermons about death: "Now that she's gone to be with God in his kingdom . . . ," a preacher might say, or "Someday we'll see those streets paved with gold in God's kingdom." Used in this way, "the kingdom of God" is a place where God reigns supreme and all the things that are wrong with this world are healed or fixed. It's that perfect place where we go when we die. The second idea is used widely to envision increased membership or expanded church activities, especially around stewardship season: "Let's build up God's kingdom together . . ." "That God's kingdom may be extended even further . . ." Sometimes that kingdom building involves the construction of a new education wing, and sometimes it refers to acts of charity and outreach, but in either case it's an activity of the congregation supported by cash. Interestingly, none of the preachers claims to have been *taught* to think about the kingdom of God this way in seminary; it seems to be simply a matter of colloquial usage.

The liturgical life of the mainstream denominations reinforces these twin associations of death and church growth with the

kingdom of God. Look at these forms for the Prayers of the People
from the Episcopal *Book of Common Prayer* (1976):

Form III
We praise you for your saints who have entered into joy;
May we also come to share in your heavenly kingdom.

Form IV
We commend to your mercy all who have died, that your will for
them may be fulfilled; and we pray that we may share with all
your saints in your eternal kingdom.

Form VI
We pray for all who have died, that they may have a place in
your eternal kingdom. Lord, let your loving-kindness be upon
them;
Who put their trust in you.[1]

All three references to the kingdom come in the petitions for
the dead. Other prayers portray the kingdom as the church:

For the choice of fit persons for the ministry
O God, you led your holy apostles to ordain ministers in every
place: Grant that your Church, under the guidance of the Holy
Spirit, may choose suitable persons for the ministry of Word and
Sacrament, and may uphold them in their work for the extension
of your kingdom; through him who is the Shepherd and Bishop
of our souls, Jesus Christ our Lord, who lives and reigns with
you and the Holy Spirit, one God, for ever and ever. *Amen.*[2]

Of a Missionary
Almighty and everlasting God, we thank you for your servant
N., whom you called to preach the Gospel to the people of —
———— (*or* to the ———— people). Raise up in this and
every land evangelists and heralds of your kingdom, that your
Church may proclaim the unsearchable riches of our Savior Jesus Christ; who lives and reigns with you and the Holy Spirit,
one God, now and for ever. *Amen.*[3]

The Presbyterian *Book of Order* displays similar uses of the phrase:

> It belongs to Christ alone to rule, to teach, to call, and to use the Church as he wills, exercising his authority by the ministry of women and men for the establishment and extension of his Kingdom.[4]

Churches of many denominations sing hymn texts like these:

I love thy kingdom, Lord, the house of thine abode,
the Church our blest Redeemer saved with his own precious
    blood.

> Timothy Dwight, 1800

The Church of God a kingdom is, where Christ in power doth
    reign,
Where spirits yearn till, seen in bliss, their Lord shall come again.

> Lionel B. C. L. Muirhead, 1899

In the New Testament, however, where the phrase "kingdom of God" (*basileia tou theou*) or Matthew's more reverential "kingdom of heaven" (*basileia ton ouranon*) is used no less than 125 times,[5] it *never* means either life after death or the visible, institutional church or its activities. It *never* means a future hope, and it *never* means something human beings can influence or contribute to. In the synoptic gospels and the Acts of the Apostles, where the bulk of the references occur (111 out of 125), the kingdom of God seems to describe a system of earthly government in which God rules directly, rather than King Herod, the Emperor Augustus, or any other contemporary head of state. As Jack Nelson-Pallmeyer, a professor of peace and justice studies at St. Thomas University, puts it succinctly, "The kingdom of God is present on earth whenever life accurately reflects the will and sovereignty of God. It is the way life and society would be if a compassionate God were in charge or imitated instead of Roman governors, client kings and the Temple establishment."[6] "The kingdom of God" is one of the most widely used phrases remembered to have come from the lips

of Jesus, and it is a key petition of the prayer he taught his followers: "Your kingdom come. Your will be done, on earth as it is in
heaven" (Matt. 6:10, Luke 11:2). Nevertheless, even among the
synoptics, the parables and images of the kingdom show consider-
able diversity. Members of the communities that produced these
gospels may have had a coherent idea about the kingdom of God,
but the definition of that kingdom differs from gospel to gospel.
The concept is at once central and elusive.

The remaining fourteen references—from the Gospel of John,
Romans, 1 Corinthians, Galatians, Colossians, 2 Thessalonians,
and Revelation—seem to refer to a mystical state to which believers
gain access through faith in the risen Christ or participation in the
baptized life; or, in the Revelation to John, to an entirely eschatological reality. The evolution of the phrase from the time of Jesus
to the period of the writing of the New Testament is worthy of several doctoral dissertations, but for my purposes, the fact that the
overwhelming preponderance of references to the kingdom of God
occur in the synoptic gospels means that I will focus my attention
there. When the synoptic Jesus sends the first missional preachers to
"proclaim the kingdom of God," just what is he asking them to do?

The Kingdom: Now or Later?

Jesus came to Galilee, proclaiming the good news of God, and
saying, "The time is fulfilled, and the kingdom of God has come
near; repent, and believe in the good news."

Mark 1:14-15

From that time Jesus began to proclaim, "Repent, for the kingdom of heaven has come near."

Matthew 4:17

[Jesus] said to them, "I must proclaim the good news of the
kingdom of God to the other cities also; for I was sent for this
purpose."

Luke 4:43

The proclamation of the kingdom of God inaugurates Jesus's public ministry in each of the synoptic gospels. It thus contextualizes everything to follow: teachings, healings, exorcisms, confrontations with representatives of the Jewish and Roman religious and political authorities, suffering, death, and resurrection. The whole story of Jesus illustrates the mysterious proclamation of the reign of God come near. While John the Baptist speaks of "one who is to come," Jesus declares the end of anticipation, not by identifying himself as the long-awaited messiah but by demonstrating how to live the messianic age—the kingdom of God—in the midst of an oppressive and discouraging reality. The fresh understandings of what Jesus's first audience might have understood by the announcement of the reign of God are captured by these passages from Horsley and Silberman's *The Message and the Kingdom:*

Here is our main hypothesis about the Galilean phase of Jesus's public career: he directly addressed the painful specifics of peasant life under the rule of Herod Antipas, offering his listeners far more than just generalized promises or threats. In Jesus's presence or under his influence, people who had been previously paralyzed or crippled by forces beyond their control began to piece their lives back together, for he offered them both a new feeling of community and a new personal confidence.[7]

Jesus taught that Israel's non-kingly Kingdom could already be present and functioning in the land's fields, towns and villages—if only people recognized its sanctity and reoriented their community life accordingly.[8]

Villagers who could have cooperated in their own liberation were at each others' throats. Jesus's healings and teachings must be therefore seen in this context, not as abstract spiritual truths spoken between stunning miracles but as a program of community action and practical resistance to a system that efficiently transformed close-knit villages into badly fragmented communities of alienated, frightened individuals. Such cooperation and mutual assistance were what the age-old covenantal tradition had fostered and articulated, and we must see these teachings as a practical response to the contemporary political and economic situation of the people of Galilee under Herodian rule.[9]

These passages follow Horsley and Silberman's exposition of the way the first King Herod (Herod the Great) and his son Herod Antipas colluded with the occupying Roman empire and the temple leadership to alter the economics of Jerusalem and Galilee radically in the space of a few decades. The combination of imperial, local, and temple taxes to support grandiose building campaigns forced landowners to become tenant farmers and tenant farmers to become day laborers. Roman industrialization coopted local fishermen to become beholden suppliers of fish-processing plants owned by absentee landlords. The audiences to whom Jesus spoke of God's reign didn't require a spiritual Messiah but political and economic liberation, and Jesus showed them a way to achieve it by reclaiming and acting upon the promises of God's ancient covenant. As John Dominic Crossan pointed out many years ago in *The Historical Jesus*, the combination of Jesus's healings, exorcisms, and shared meals is programmatic rather than random, at once highlighting and redeeming the inequities of life for the most marginalized members of society. And, when Crossan looks at our Luke 9 commissioning of preachers of the kingdom, he sees Jesus's recruits being taught to offer the same practices more widely: shared meals and acts of healing.[10] In Horsley and Silberman's phrase, the people who hear the first missional preachers are being taught both "resistance" and "renewal." By choosing to act on the promises of God's ancient covenant with Israel without waiting for a messianic king to be crowned at Jerusalem, they are renewing their belief in their religious tradition and using it to resist present-day oppression.[11] So what Jesus was asking his preachers to do was both to announce and to enact the kingdom of God by their words, by the meals they shared, and by their acts of healing and exorcism.

The reimagining of Jesus's message in light of contemporary historical scholarship is exhilarating for some and off-putting for others. Critics of the historical Jesus movement complain that scholars like Crossan and Horsley and Silberman are recasting the Christ of faith as a political revolutionary. Supporters of the scholarship and even nonprofessional interested readers are energized by grasping for the first time why Jesus might have made the political and religious establishments of his day angry enough to kill him. For the purposes of this book we can safely steer a middle ground between these camps by simply concentrating on the scriptural record. Jesus sent preachers to proclaim the kingdom of God, and the many references to that kingdom recorded in the synoptic gospels never describe life after death or a new religious organization that will carry out charitable activities while remaining allied with the powers that be. That, after all, was the religious situation Jesus found as his public ministry began. But we still need to get a better idea of what the kingdom of God might mean today, and we need to understand the historical forces that have led us to remold the kingdom of God into a far more abstract and less dangerous idea than the one the New Testament describes.

One way to begin to parse what Jesus and his first communities of followers may have meant by "the kingdom of God"—and to see how different it is from our usage today—is to contrast the verbs preachers most often use to talk about the kingdom with those used by the New Testament itself.

By Their Verbs You Shall Know Them

When "the kingdom of God" is used to refer to life after death or the visible church and its activities, certain verbs become its natural companions: in the case of life after death, the kingdom is a place we "go to." When thinking about the kingdom of God as the visible church or its activities, preachers tend to use verbs like "build," build up," "extend," "establish," and "spread."

The first usage makes the kingdom of God a place, a location different from wherever the speaker is now; the latter makes the kingdom of God something within our grasp, something that we can enlarge and make better, something that needs our help to be noticed in the world. Each of the verbs mentioned above has a Greek equivalent that occurs in the New Testament, but none of them is ever linked to the phrase "kingdom of God." What is "built" (constructed) in the New Testament is the temple, a city, a

tower, or the church;[12] what is "built up" (edified) is the church as
community of faith;[13] what is "extended" is hospitality[14] or grace;[15]
what is "established" is God's covenant;[16] and what is "spread" is
news about Jesus or the kingdom of God, not the kingdom itself.[17]
What a difference there is between "extending the kingdom" and
"extending grace"!

The verbs that are connected with the kingdom of God in the
New Testament are very different: "enter," "receive," "inherit,"
"wait for," and "proclaim" (or "preach"). The linking of these
verbs to the kingdom of God makes clear that human beings have
no role whatsoever in creating or sustaining it, much less in enlarg-
ing it or getting it noticed: it is whole and complete and comes as
a gift or bequest, and that is the only way human beings can get it.
According to the New Testament, the kingdom of God cannot be
augmented or diminished by human activity.

This news comes as a shock to the practicing clergy in my classes,
one far greater than any political rereading of Jesus's message and
ministry. "Why haven't I known this?" they ask with ashen faces.
"I've been preaching it all wrong!" As we study the hundred-plus
references to the kingdom of God in the New Testament, it becomes
evident that the way the church typically speaks about the kingdom
and the way Jesus is remembered to have spoken about it are at
odds. When we immerse ourselves in the synoptic theology of the
kingdom, we see can't help but realize that Jesus's message about
God's radical acceptance of the human race and a renewed quest
for earthly justice in response to it has been eclipsed by the institutional needs of the church. The question that invariably arises at
this stage is "What happened to the kingdom of God?"

What Happened to the Kingdom of God?

Roman Catholic theologian Thomas Sheehan took on this question
directly in his 1986 book *The First Coming: How the Kingdom of
God Became Christianity*, written as a distillation of the historical
Jesus scholarship that had emerged to date and its implications
for Christendom theology. Sheehan took readers on a step-by-step
journey from the sociopolitical setting of Jesus to the lofty proc-

lamations of the ecumenical councils, allowing them to see that evolution as all-too-human rather than divinely guided. Coming from a very different school of thought from Roland Allen, Leslie Newbigin, and David Bosch, Sheehan nevertheless anticipated the advent of missional theology by a decade by asking whatever happened to Jesus's own announcement of the reign of God come to earth. He describes three ways the church "managed" the explosive announcement of the kingdom of God:

> 1. While Jesus spoke of enacting the kingdom in justice and mercy, the church made Jesus himself the embodiment of the kingdom.
> 2. While Jesus spoke of God's future breaking in now as opportunity and judgment, the church created "salvation history," which contained and compartmentalized God's actions into comprehensible but abstract ideas.
> 3. While Jesus offered the end of religion, the church made a new religion based on Jesus.[18]

Sheehan sees these developments not as some sinister plot on the part of the emerging institutional church, but as a practically unavoidable consequence of trying to convey the message of and about Jesus to subsequent generations. In a sense, Christianity as a religion was undone by its own success, becoming a self-contained set of propositions about the nature of life and God's intervention in it by the time it had become a worldwide religion. The three points above can be seen as one great postponement of the announcement Jesus makes at the start of his public ministry in each of the synoptic gospels. Jesus spoke of the long-awaited future happening *now* and taught anyone who would listen how to live in that realized future. Rather than taking Jesus at his word and acting on his training, the church made Jesus the first and best practitioner of that training, worshiping his ability to live the truth he spoke. Jesus declared the end of waiting, but the church reinvented the waiting cycle by looking for Jesus to return at the end of history. Jesus told his followers that they didn't need to go to the temple and offer sacrifice—they could go into their rooms and shut their doors and pray in secret—but the church reinvented the temple and multiplied it throughout the world, reinforcing the idea that God requires right offerings to forgive sinners and outdoing the Sadducees and Pharisees in both ceremony and ritual laws.

This theological evolution of Jesus's message was not merely a corruption or distortion of it. As Sheehan writes, "Christianity is not a false interpretation but one possible interpretation of the meaning of the kingdom of God."[19] We see the groundwork for what becomes a normative Christian understanding in the New Testament itself:

> Long ago God spoke to our ancestors in many and various ways by the prophets, but in these last days he has spoken to us by a Son, whom he appointed heir of all things, through whom he also created the worlds. He is the reflection of God's glory and the exact imprint of God's very being, and he sustains all things by his powerful word. When he had made purification for sins, he sat down at the right hand of the Majesty on high, having become as much superior to angels as the name he has inherited is more excellent than theirs.
>
>   Hebrews 1:1-4

This passage, like many others in the New Testament, takes us far from the sociopolitical realities in the midst of which Jesus proclaimed the reign of God present on earth. The mythological pattern of a redeemer who descends from heaven and then returns again underlies this passage and accomplishes all three points of the Sheehan argument cited above. It makes Jesus himself the focus of God's action, moves Jesus out of time into eternity, and lays the groundwork for a stable institution that can present the story of redemption with a beginning, middle, and end. The perpetual problem with this kind of interpretation of the meaning of Jesus, however, is the feeling of lethargy it bestows on congregations. So complete is the redemption accomplished by Jesus that subsequent generations can only respond with awe and intellectual assent to so great a gift. And, indeed, for many centuries, preachers have understood themselves as "sent" to tell this very story and to evoke both that assent and that awe in listening congregations. I was such a preacher myself until the day when my five-year-old parishioner made me question whether I was engaged in a perpetual loop of informing and persuading.

The missional preachers sent by Jesus to proclaim the reign of God and to heal seem to have evoked more than awe and intellectual assent from their listeners: some of their audiences wanted them to get out of town, and Jesus told them to be prepared for that response. If contemporary preachers take seriously a proclamation of the reign of God that is not about a place you go to when you die or the expansion of the institutional church and its activities, they might well prepare themselves for a similar response. But we have the cart before the horse. Is it even possible for contemporary preachers to re-engage the proclamation of the reign of God? If so, how would they do it and what would that proclamation sound like?

Reimagining the Reign of God

The only way to begin this journey is to immerse ourselves in the synoptic gospels with a fresh eye to language about the reign of God. What we begin to see when we look at the texts this way is that each of the gospels emerges as a portrait of the missional understanding of the community that created it: "Here is what we have been sent to do." It is both hermeneutically sound and eminently practical to consider the images of the kingdom of God gospel by gospel rather than individually, because each particular community's sense of mission shapes the selection and presentation of those images. In the following pages I offer the reader the same exercise I offer students in the classroom. There I present the combined references to the kingdom of God in a given gospel and ask students to gather in small groups to discuss together what they notice about these references. No commentaries are permitted for this work—not because of any anti-intellectual bias but because the commentaries are shaped by a variety of agendas not applicable to a simple response to language choice. I ask my students to use their intuitive and associative minds rather than their cognitive and analytical ones. I invite you to do the same as you read through these lists. See what you notice about each gospel's description of the kingdom.

The Markan Community

Mark 1:14-15: Jesus came to Galilee, proclaiming the good news of God, and saying, "The time is fulfilled, and the kingdom of God has come near; repent, and believe in the good news."

Mark 4:11: And he said to them, "To you has been given the secret of the kingdom of God, but for those outside, everything comes in parables . . ."

Mark 4:26-27: "The kingdom of God is as if someone would scatter seed on the ground, and would sleep and rise night and day, and the seed would sprout and grow, he does not know how."

Mark 4:30: He also said, "With what can we compare the kingdom of God, or what parable will we use for it? It is like a mustard seed, which, when sown upon the ground, is the smallest of all the seeds on earth; yet when it is sown it grows up and becomes the greatest of all shrubs, and puts forth large branches, so that the birds of the air can make nests in its shade."

Mark 9:1: And he said to them, "Truly I tell you, there are some standing here who will not taste death until they see that the kingdom of God has come with power."

Mark 9:47: "And if your eye causes you to stumble, tear it out; it is better for you to enter the kingdom of God with one eye than to have two eyes and to be thrown into hell."

Mark 10:14: But when Jesus saw this, he was indignant and said to them, "Let the little children come to me; do not stop them; for it is to such as these that the kingdom of God belongs."

Mark 10:15: "Truly I tell you, whoever does not receive the kingdom of God as a little child will never enter it."

Mark 10:23: Then Jesus looked around and said to his disciples, "How hard it will be for those who have wealth to enter the kingdom of God!"

Mark 10:24: And the disciples were perplexed at these words. But Jesus said to them again, "Children, how hard it is to enter the kingdom of God! It is easier for a camel to go

through the eye of a needle than for someone who is rich
to enter the kingdom of God."

Mark 12:34: When Jesus saw that he answered wisely, he said
to him, "You are not far from the kingdom of God."

Mark 14:25: "Truly I tell you, I will never again drink of the
fruit of the vine until that day when I drink it new in the
kingdom of God."

Mark 15:43: Joseph of Arimathea, a respected member of the
council, who was also himself waiting expectantly for the
kingdom of God, went boldly to Pilate and asked for the
body of Jesus.

Students have varying degrees of difficulty letting go of commentaries and sharing their immediate and direct responses to each
of these references to the kingdom of God. Some find it liberating,
some frustrating; but the lists they produce of their observations
are always rich and revelatory. Here is a sample of student responses synthesized from several years of classes responding to the
preceding list of Markan references:

The kingdom of God can be near or far.
You can go into the kingdom.
The kingdom is hard for some to go into, easy for others.
The kingdom grows like magic.
The kingdom can be pointed to.
The kingdom is mysterious.
The kingdom is for the innocent, the simple, and children.
The kingdom is costly.
The kingdom is a refuge or home.
The kingdom puts you in conflict with the status quo.
The kingdom is powerful.
The kingdom is uncomfortable for the rich.
The kingdom is expanding.

Assuming Mark as the basis for the other two synoptic gospels, we might expect the references to the kingdom of God to
be similar in Matthew and Luke. They are and are not; a distinct
vision of the kingdom emerges from the additional references and
nuances of language in each.

The Matthean Community

Matthew 3:2: "Repent, for the kingdom of heaven has come near."

Matthew 4:17: From that time Jesus began to proclaim, "Repent, for the kingdom of heaven has come near."

Matthew 4:23: Jesus went throughout Galilee, teaching in their synagogues and proclaiming the good news of the kingdom and curing every disease and every sickness among the people.

Matthew 5:3: "Blessed are the poor in spirit, for theirs is the kingdom of heaven."

Matthew 5:10: "Blessed are those who are persecuted for righteousness' sake, for theirs is the kingdom of heaven."

Matthew 5:19: "Therefore, whoever breaks one of the least of these commandments, and teaches others to do the same, will be called least in the kingdom of heaven; but whoever does them and teaches them will be called great in the kingdom of heaven."

Matthew 5:20: "For I tell you, unless your righteousness exceeds that of the scribes and Pharisees, you will never enter the kingdom of heaven."

Matthew 6:10: "Your kingdom come. Your will be done, on earth as it is in heaven."

Matthew 6:33: "But strive first for the kingdom of God and his righteousness, and all these things will be given to you as well."

Matthew 7:21: "Not everyone who says to me, 'Lord, Lord,' will enter the kingdom of heaven, but only the one who does the will of my Father in heaven."

Matthew 8:11: "I tell you, many will come from east and west and will eat with Abraham and Isaac and Jacob in the kingdom of heaven."

Matthew 9:35: Then Jesus went about all the cities and villages, teaching in their synagogues, and proclaiming the good news of the kingdom, and curing every disease and every sickness.

Matthew 10:7: "As you go, proclaim the good news, 'The kingdom of heaven has come near.'"

Matthew 11:11: "Truly I tell you, among those born of women no one has arisen greater than John the Baptist; yet the least in the kingdom of heaven is greater than he."

Matthew 11:12: "From the days of John the Baptist until now the kingdom of heaven has suffered violence, and the violent take it by force."

Matthew 12:28: "But if it is by the Spirit of God that I cast out demons, then the kingdom of God has come to you."

Matthew 13:11: He answered, "To you it has been given to know the secrets of the kingdom of heaven, but to them it has not been given."

Matthew 13:24: He put before them another parable: "The kingdom of heaven may be compared to someone who sowed good seed in his field . . ."

Matthew 13:31: He put before them another parable: "The kingdom of heaven is like a mustard seed that someone took and sowed in his field . . ."

Matthew 13:33: He told them another parable: "The kingdom of heaven is like yeast that a woman took and mixed in with three measures of flour until all of it was leavened."

Matthew 13:44: "The kingdom of heaven is like treasure hidden in a field, which someone found and hid; then in his joy he goes and sells all that he has and buys that field."

Matthew 13:45: "Again, the kingdom of heaven is like a merchant in search of fine pearls; on finding one pearl of great value, he went and sold all that he had and bought it."

Matthew 13:47: "Again, the kingdom of heaven is like a net that was thrown into the sea and caught fish of every kind . . ."

Matthew 13:52: And he said to them, "Therefore every scribe who has been trained for the kingdom of heaven is like the master of a household who brings out of his treasure what is new and what is old."

Matthew 16:19: "I will give you the keys of the kingdom of heaven, and whatever you bind on earth will be bound in heaven, and whatever you loose on earth will be loosed in heaven."

Matthew 18:1: At that time the disciples came to Jesus and asked, "Who is the greatest in the kingdom of heaven?"

Matthew 18:3: "Truly I tell you, unless you change and become like children, you will never enter the kingdom of heaven."

Matthew 18:4: "Whoever becomes humble like this child is the greatest in the kingdom of heaven."

Matthew 18:23: "For this reason the kingdom of heaven may be compared to a king who wished to settle accounts with his slaves . . ."

Matthew 19:12: "For there are eunuchs who have been so from birth, and there are eunuchs who have been made eunuchs by others, and there are eunuchs who have made themselves eunuchs for the sake of the kingdom of heaven."

Matthew 19:14: "Let the little children come to me, and do not stop them; for it is to such as these that the kingdom of heaven belongs."

Matthew 19:23: Then Jesus said to his disciples, "Truly I tell you, it will be hard for a rich person to enter the kingdom of heaven."

Matthew 19:24: "Again I tell you, it is easier for a camel to go through the eye of a needle than for someone who is rich to enter the kingdom of God."

Matthew 20:1: "For the kingdom of heaven is like a landowner who went out early in the morning to hire laborers for his vineyard."

Matthew 21:31: "Which of the two did the will of his father?" They said, "The first." Jesus said to them, "Truly I tell you, the tax collectors and the prostitutes are going into the kingdom of God ahead of you."

Matthew 21:43: "Therefore I tell you, the kingdom of God will be taken away from you and given to a people that produces the fruits of the kingdom."

Matthew 22:2: "The kingdom of heaven may be compared to a king who gave a wedding banquet for his son. . ."

Matthew 23:13: "But woe to you, scribes and Pharisees, hypocrites! For you lock people out of the kingdom of heaven. For you do not go in yourselves, and when others are going in, you stop them."

Matthew 24:14: "And this good news of the kingdom will be proclaimed throughout the world, as a testimony to all the nations; and then the end will come."

Matthew 25:1: "Then the kingdom of heaven will be like this. Ten bridesmaids took their lamps and went to meet the bridegroom . . ."

Matthew 25:34: "Then the king will say to those at his right hand, 'Come, you that are blessed by my Father, inherit the kingdom prepared for you from the foundation of the world.'"

Matthew 26:29: "I tell you, I will never again drink of this fruit of the vine until that day when I drink it new with you in my Father's kingdom."

And the synthesis of student observations of this list:

The kingdom is near and/or close to us.
You can be inside the kingdom or outside it.
There are behavioral expectations of the kingdom.
The kingdom gives priority to those on the margins.
The kingdom looks like a just society.
People can be locked out or let into the kingdom.
The kingdom requires change.
The kingdom can be taught.
There is rank in the kingdom, but not like rank elsewhere.
The kingdom has a place for the persecuted.
The kingdom is highly valuable but also highly common, ordinary.

The Lukan Community

Luke 4:43: But he said to them, "I must proclaim the good news of the kingdom of God to the other cities also; for I was sent for this purpose."

Luke 6:20: Then he looked up at his disciples and said: "Blessed are you who are poor, for yours is the kingdom of God."

Luke 7:28: "I tell you, among those born of women no one is greater than John; yet the least in the kingdom of God is greater than he."

Luke 8:1: Soon afterwards he went on through cities and villages, proclaiming and bringing the good news of the kingdom of God.

Luke 8:10: He said, "To you it has been given to know the secrets of the kingdom of God; but to others I speak in parables, so that 'looking they may not perceive, and listening they may not understand.'"

Luke 9:1-2: Then Jesus called the twelve together and gave them power and authority over all demons and to cure diseases, and he sent them out to proclaim the kingdom of God and to heal.

Luke 9:11: When the crowds found out about it, they followed him; and he welcomed them, and spoke to them about the kingdom of God, and healed those who needed to be cured.

Luke 9:27: "But truly I tell you, there are some standing here who will not taste death before they see the kingdom of God."

Luke 9:60: But Jesus said to him, "Let the dead bury their own dead; but as for you, go and proclaim the kingdom of God."

Luke 9:62: Jesus said to him, "No one who puts a hand to the plow and looks back is fit for the kingdom of God."

Luke 10:9-11: "Whenever you enter a town and its people welcome you, eat what is set before you; cure the sick who are there, and say to them, 'The kingdom of God has come near to you.' But whenever you enter a town and they do not welcome you, go out into its streets and say, 'Even the dust of your town that clings to our feet, we wipe off in protest against you. Yet know this: the kingdom of God has come near.' I tell you, on that day it will be more tolerable for Sodom than for that town."

Luke 11:2: He said to them, "When you pray, say: Father, hallowed be your name. Your kingdom come."

Luke 11:20: "But if it is by the finger of God that I cast out the demons, then the kingdom of God has come to you."

Luke 12:31: "Instead, strive for his kingdom, and these things will be given to you as well."

Luke 12:32: "Do not be afraid, little flock, for it is your Father's good pleasure to give you the kingdom."

Luke 13:18-19: He said therefore, "What is the kingdom of God like? And to what should I compare it? It is like a mustard seed that someone took and sowed in the garden; it grew and became a tree, and the birds of the air made nests in its branches."

Luke 13:20: And again he said, "To what should I compare the kingdom of God? It is like yeast that a woman took and mixed in with three measures of flour until all of it was leavened."

Luke 13:28-29: "There will be weeping and gnashing of teeth when you see Abraham and Isaac and Jacob and all the prophets in the kingdom of God, and you yourselves thrown out. Then people will come from east and west, from north and south, and will eat in the kingdom of God."

Luke 14:15: One of the dinner guests, on hearing this, said to him, "Blessed is anyone who will eat bread in the kingdom of God!"

Luke 16:16: "The law and the prophets were in effect until John came; since then the good news of the kingdom of God is proclaimed, and everyone tries to enter it by force."

Luke 17:20: Once Jesus was asked by the Pharisees when the kingdom of God was coming, and he answered, "The kingdom of God is not coming with things that can be observed; nor will they say, 'Look, here it is!' or 'There it is!' For, in fact, the kingdom of God is among you."

Luke 18:16-17: But Jesus called for them and said, "Let the little children come to me, and do not stop them; for it is to such as these that the kingdom of God belongs. Truly I tell you, whoever does not receive the kingdom of God as a little child will never enter it."

Luke 18:24-25: Jesus looked at him and said, "How hard it is for those who have wealth to enter the kingdom of God! Indeed, it is easier for a camel to go through the eye of a needle than for someone who is rich to enter the kingdom of God."

Luke 18:29-30: "Truly I tell you, there is no one who has left house or wife or brothers or parents or children, for the

sake of the kingdom of God, who will not get back very
much more in this age, and in the age to come eternal
life."

Luke 19:11: As they were listening to this, he went on to tell
a parable, because he was near Jerusalem, and because
they supposed that the kingdom of God was to appear
immediately.

Luke 21:31: "So also, when you see these things taking place,
you know that the kingdom of God is near."

Luke 22:16: "For I tell you, I will not eat it until it is fulfilled
in the kingdom of God."

Luke 22:18: "For I tell you that from now on I will not drink
of the fruit of the vine until the kingdom of God comes."

Luke 22:29: ". . . and I confer on you, just as my Father has
conferred on me, a kingdom."

Luke 22:30: ". . . so that you may eat and drink at my table
in my kingdom, and you will sit on thrones judging the
twelve tribes of Israel."

Luke 23:51: He came from the Jewish town of Arimathea, and
he was waiting expectantly for the kingdom of God.

And the synthesis of student observations:

The kingdom takes precedence over routine life.
The kingdom is hospitable.
The kingdom is inclusive.
The kingdom is unexpectedly bountiful.
The kingdom is near in time and space.
The kingdom makes demands on those who enter it.
It's important to bring nothing with you into the kingdom.

For most of my students it is unusual to look at the synoptic
gospels through the lens of the reign of God. While most have
been exposed to parallel editions of the gospels, few have followed
a single concept across all three unless it was for a particular exegesis paper. The result of this exercise is the realization that the
communities that produced the synoptic gospels had particular
understandings of the kingdom of God and what it looked like in

their midst—what kind of behavior it required and how it might
be lived out on earth. In the subtly different presentations of the
manifestations of the kingdom offered by each of the synoptic gospels, we get a glimpse of how each of those communities understood its missional identity: what each was sent to be and do. The
distinctive stamp put on the concept of the kingdom of God by
each gospel community prevents any easy synthesis or final definition of what the three accounts mean by "the kingdom," but
it does invite the possibility that present-day Christian communities might engage in a similar process of naming the kingdom of
God in the images and experiences familiar to them. As George
Hunsberger, one of the authors of *Missional Church,* points out
in chapter 4 of that book, "The church may adhere too strictly to
scriptural forms of expressing its faith that were intelligible to the
cultures of biblical times, and in the process neglect to translate
the biblical warrant into an incarnation relevant to the church's
current time and place."[20]

And so the second part of the process of reimagining the
kingdom of God is to engage in a similar act of imagination
for ourselves and the communities in which we preach. How
would we name the reign of God? What would it look like for us
personally, communally, and globally? What is the missional identity of our community? What are we sent to do? To stimulate
answers to these questions I distribute a handout headed by the
quote from Jack Nelson-Pallmeyer cited above, and adding these
questions:

Imagining the Kingdom of God Exercise
Jesus says the kingdom of God is present on earth whenever life
accurately reflects the will and sovereignty of God. It is the way
life and society would be if a compassionate God were in charge
or imitated instead of Roman governors, client kings and the
Temple establishment.[21]

In light of this statement:

What would the kingdom of God look like in your own life?
What would the kingdom of God look like in your
community's life?

What would the kingdom of God look like in the world?

Some students plunge into this exercise with gusto and can answer the questions quickly and vividly. Others feel stymied by the task, trying to match a concept they didn't hear much about in seminary to the daily life of the communities they serve and the world in which they live. But over the course of the semester everyone's list takes shape and reflects the unity and diversity of the gospel images themselves. They range from the quirkily personal ("The kingdom of God is like coming back from the ladies' room in a fancy restaurant and dancing the whole evening with toilet paper stuck to your shoe") to the keenly observed ("The kingdom of God is like Hanna cutting her own hair in Sunday school and putting it on her picture of Jesus") to the revolutionary ("The kingdom of God is like the INS throwing a welcome party with green cards as confetti").

As we listen to each other's lists, our imaginations expand, and we also become more discerning about what we are doing. On the one hand, by listening to one another we gain a multitude of new ideas about what the kingdom of God might be or look like in personal, communal, and global contexts. On the other hand, we become more discriminating about the ways our ideas reflect or do not reflect the kingdom of God as it is presented by the synoptic gospels. We become self-corrective about items on our lists that simply represent "a few of our favorite things," sources of pleasure or happiness that can quickly reveal the privileged status of the list maker. For instance, with two-thirds of the world undernourished or starving, does a strawberry ice-cream cone on a hot summer day truly reveal the reign of God? Well, yes and no. If that ice-cream cone were the horizon of our vision of God's reign, it would be pretty limited. But to the extent that God's reign on earth might be like relief, refreshment, and delight, that image might be the start of a deeper meditation.

As we move on from the personal level to imagining the kingdom of God in our cities (affordable housing?), nation (true racial equity?), and world (a universally adequate food supply?), this exercise also helps us distinguish between even our most cherished political platforms and the reign of God on earth. After all, there are good arguments for achieving a just society quite apart from striving to be faithful to the mission of God in history. In many times and places the church may have erred on the side of proclaiming an entirely spiritualized message. Nevertheless, a church that has made a renewed commitment to justice and solidarity can claim integrity only if that commitment comes in response to a just God who is already in solidarity with the human race. Missional preaching can't just offer the New Deal with hymns. It must point to the work of a God who is more interested in reconciliation than increased membership in any organization.

I always ask my students to be as specific as possible as they imagine the reign of God in their communities, like the Gospel of Luke's John the Baptist when the crowds respond to his preaching with the question "What then should we do?" He replies: "Whoever has two coats must share with anyone who has none; and whoever has food must do likewise." To tax collectors he says, "Collect no more than the amount prescribed for you," and to soldiers, "Do not extort money from anyone by threats or false accusations and be satisfied with your wages." (Luke 3:10-14). The degree to which preachers can hold up images of the reign of God made flesh in local places, names, and activities ("The kingdom of God is like Marian and Genevieve trading their secret recipes for cranberry nut bread at last year's Christmas bazaar and never telling anyone . . .") will be the degree to which such images can function proleptically, allowing listeners to experience God's future now, and thus begin to make concrete choices that move them toward that future in hope and anticipation.

If congregations can see, hear, smell, and taste the kingdom of God, they can begin to sense the possibility of what it would mean to choose to enter or receive it. When the kingdom of God is no longer the place you go when you die or a successful stewardship campaign but the redeeming activity of God in the world, holy imagining can begin. If freeing the preachers from those constraints results in a new sense of joy and purpose in the pulpit, what if whole congregations began reshaping their idea of God's reign come among them—no longer waiting to get there after death or writing a check to try to build it now? As exciting as the possibilities may be, we can't just speak about the reign of God to congregations formed by sermons about the maintenance of Christendom and expect them to be transformed overnight. Just like the first audiences of missional preaching, contemporary listeners need to recover a sense of agency to be able to respond to the proclamation of the reign of God.

CHAPTER 5

Reimagining the Congregation

Even after years of ordained ministry and seminary teaching, I find it remarkable that some combination of the ordination process and theological education consistently produces a preaching event that's a hybrid of a beauty contest, a piano recital, and a competitive sporting event. Preachers worry about their sermons. They want them to be good, even excellent, both meaningful and helpful, challenging and uplifting. But very few preachers can avoid viewing their sermons as a referendum on their overall worth as human beings and the degree to which they are liked and supported by their listeners. Like performers in other fields, they fear the reviews. A few brave souls conduct regular talk-backs at coffee hour. More than a few join clergy peer groups to discuss and evaluate their preaching. But most rest content with a handshake and "Thanks for your message" at the church door on Sunday morning, relieved that no one seemed too upset on the days when the sermon had an edge.

This was not the kind of response Jesus anticipated for the first preachers he sent to proclaim the kingdom of God and heal the sick. "If anyone receives you," Jesus says, "do this." "If anyone refuses to receive you, do this." If the gospel is universally good news that everyone should want to know and embrace, why does Jesus give instructions on how to bail? As we saw in the previous chapter, the announcement of an alternative to the domination systems of the temple, Herod, and the Roman Empire was inevitably controversial. But because Jesus offered an alternative to these systems of coercion, he necessarily had to use different tactics: listeners had to have a genuine choice about whether to receive the reign of God. The choices most sermon audiences are given are usually far more modest: whether to listen, whether to give money to the cause mentioned, whether to participate in a church activity. Of course, preachers in the evangelical tradition frequently offer life-changing choices that seem far from modest: accept Jesus as your personal savior; choose heaven as a destination rather than hell. Some might say that these are opportunities to choose the reign of God, but our analysis of missional preaching thus far does not support that conclusion. The preachers sent by Jesus did not proclaim his lordship, or membership in a new religious organization, or choices concerning the afterlife. They proclaimed the kingdom of God. Those who chose the sovereignty of the God of justice were making both a personal and a social choice. By opting out of the domination systems of Jerusalem and Rome, they were free to begin a very different kind of life. While we could certainly see Jesus's instructions to his preachers as a kind of implied threat to their audiences, I'm struck by the fact that Jesus assumes that listeners should have a choice about whether to receive the proclamation: they have agency, the ability to act.

Michael Warren, a Roman Catholic educator and theologian, has written an entire book about congregations and agency. In *At This Time, In This Place: The Spirit Embodied in the Local Assembly,* Warren offers an extended analysis of the ways Vatican II did and did not restore agency to local congregations through its monumental changes in Roman Catholic liturgy and language. In a chapter titled "How We Speak in the Church" he writes:

> If religious inarticulateness is actually a common feature of many religious people today, then the practice of the local church somehow fosters it in ways too often overlooked. My underlying conviction is that the potential of the church to be a sign of good news will not be realized unless the conditions of speaking in the local assembly are changed. Where the people of a local church exercise little social and cultural agency, it is a sign that

the procedures of that local assembly actively, though in many cases unwittingly, foster passivity.[1]

Warren uses two easily recognizable metaphors to describe behavior in worship: houseguest and family member. When we are guests in someone's home, especially for the first time, we don't go around opening doors or looking into closets if we find we need extra towels; we ask our host to show us where to find them, or perhaps wait to receive them directly from our host. Family members, on the other hand, know where to look for the extra towels, and howl when the supply runs out. Warren describes the situation this way:

> The position of "the people" in many local churches is like that of a houseguest, warmly welcomed but made aware of her proper place in the household. Her welcome is connected to a series of unspoken rules: Do not critique the polity of the household by commenting on the parenting practices or housekeeping skills of the hosts. Enjoy your stay here but know your place—and know, especially, that this is not your place. Such unspoken rules demarcate the limits of a houseguest's agency.[2]

The moment I read those words I finally understood why the phrase "Please be seated" has always rubbed me the wrong way when used in worship, from the time I joined the church as a teenager through years of ordained ministry. Think of the power relationship encoded in that simple phrase! When I've brought this concern up with colleagues, it's usually dismissed as a way to help visitors know what to do, but I'm not so sure. Family members don't wait for an invitation to sit down; if it's time to eat or watch television, the family simply gathers and sits down. If the members of the congregation felt at home in their own worship space, they would sit down at the moments the liturgy expects it, and visitors would easily follow suit. In fact, however, liturgically oriented congregations will often go on standing indefinitely, even when they know it's time to sit down, if the words "please be seated" have been omitted by the leader of worship.

People who wait to be told to sit down can hardly be expected to glimpse the reign of God proclaimed in sermon form and choose to take its privileges and responsibilities upon themselves overnight. As innocuous as it may seem, the "please be seated" character of Christian worship represents the fruit of centuries of formation that placed all the agency in the hands of the ordained. Thus it would be quite possible for clergy to read half this book and get excited about preaching the reign of God while ignoring the ways their local church's practice may invalidate their newly focused message. The agency Jesus's first missional preachers expected in their listeners must first be restored to contemporary congregations.

The idea of a congregation's agency is rarely the subject of seminary education, which typically overlooks the agency of seminarians as well. Like other kinds of graduate school, seminary education by and large maintains a top-down system of training experts to dispense knowledge to those who lack it. The fairly recent trend in homiletics of building behavioral outcomes into sermon construction is an exception to this generality, though in my experience the behaviors hoped for remain modest and somewhat churchified: "I want people to experience the love of God" or "I want people to participate in our food pantry." That people will love God and feed the poor are both noble goals for sermons, but they assume that the sermon will do little to change the status quo of the world outside the church. Could the congregation become a "sign of the gospel" by taking on the conditions in its local community that make the food pantry a necessity? It's not just a question of proposing more ambitious programs. It's a question of preaching in a way that allows listeners to claim agency in their respective spheres, acting *as* the church rather than doing things *for* the church. Can contemporary Christians hear the reign of God proclaimed and choose it for themselves and their society as the listeners to Jesus's first missional preachers did?

One of the most stultifying forces working against such agency is an old saw that virtually every Christian preacher seems to have picked up from seminary, or a book, or the air: "Comfort the afflicted and afflict the comfortable"—a formula for maintenance preaching if ever there was one, portraying a world divided into fixed stereotypes of fortune and misfortune, one group helpless and the other indifferent! And yet the phrase is repeated constantly as though it carried scriptural authority.[3] How this sarcastic description of a newspaper's role penned by Chicago journalist Finley Peter Dunne in 1900 became a description of preaching is a mystery, even in the age of Internet searches, but it has had remarkable staying power.[4] Why does it hold such appeal for so many? Perhaps it contains the seed of an aspiration many preachers have for their sermons—that they will indeed have an effect on the rich and powerful and bring about transformation in an unjust society. But theological education trains clergy to comfort the afflicted far more effectively than it prepares them to afflict the comfortable, though many new clergy arrive in their first pulpits with a naive prejudice against the rich. This prejudice rarely matures into a nuanced critique of money and power and how the two both enable or prevent agency, because clergy are by and large forced to become fundraisers, an assignment that puts constraints upon any preaching deemed "political." The resulting tension is all the more remarkable given the gospel portraits of Jesus's equal-opportunity interactions with virtually every stratum of his tightly organized society.

Bounded vs. Centered Sets, Then and Now

The eighth chapter of Guder's *Missional Church* offers a helpful way of thinking about congregations and agency by borrowing from set theory. (Don't panic! There's no actual math involved.) Bounded sets are those we belong to because we've acknowledged and crossed some kind of line of demarcation to get there. "How do I become a member of this church?" people ask, both at the local and denominational levels. "How do I join this congregation?" "How do I become a Methodist, a Lutheran, or a Roman Catholic?" The answers often involve agreeing to a set of written tenets and participating in some kind of initiation rite, from a formal confirmation to a casual welcome of new members at a Sunday service. Of course, Christianity itself exists as a bounded set entered through baptism and, in most of its expressions, through admission to the Eucharist. Nevertheless, the approximately 35,000 groups calling themselves Christians[5] have nearly as many rules and procedures for becoming a part of their particular bounded sets. Within memory, many North American Christians could easily identify themselves by the bounded sets they hailed from: "My parents were Wisconsin Synod Lutherans, but I married a Southern Baptist, and we decided to become Presbyterians together." In the past two generations, however, this kind of denominational identity has weakened as many Americans who would readily identify themselves as Christian are less certain about which branch of Christianity they belong to or what that means. In the age of church shopping, people seeking a "church home" have demonstrated themselves more than willing to treat denominational boundaries as porous in their quest for a meaningful worship experience or programs for their families. And so, increasingly, the bounded set in question is not a communion or a denomination but a local congregation. "We are the people who belong to First Church." Everyone on the parish rolls could be considered a member of that set.

You belong to a bounded set by virtue of meeting the entrance requirements or by crossing some sort of threshold that puts you in that set. Belonging to a bounded set may or may not require any further activity on your part to maintain or live out your membership. By contrast, a centered set is formed by people who have a common purpose and who choose to band together to accomplish it. They may come from a variety of bounded sets, but their shared commitment to achieving a goal or living out a principle makes of them a new set that transcends their bounded-set identities. To quote *Missional Church*:

> The centered-set organization invites people to enter on a journey toward a set of values and commitments. For example, in the model that we have been developing in this book, the direction toward which people would be invited to move is the gospel's announcement of God's reign that is forming a people as God's new society.[6]

This distinction between faith community as bounded set or centered set is by no means a contemporary phenomenon, however. We see it in the public ministry of Jesus, the calling of the disciples, and the formation of Christian communities in the first centuries of the Common Era.

The Second Temple, vastly enlarged and beautified by Herod the Great over a forty-year period, provided a blueprint of the bounded sets by which Israel's identity was established. It was one of the wonders of the ancient world, and people came from throughout the Mediterranean world and Asia just to see it. A large perimeter wall established the temple precinct, and the broad plaza inside that wall but not yet inside any of these gates was identified as the Court of the Gentiles. You may have come from as far as Spain or Persia to see Israel's temple, but if you were not a Jew, you could advance no further than that court. This is a bit curious, because any priest or teacher of the Law in Jesus's time would have told you that the God of Israel was not a local or tribal God but the creator of the world and the God of all people on the face of the globe. The Jewish community was open to and even zealous for converts, yet at the heart of that community was the temple in Jerusalem, and its architecture was a map of the way this universal theology was actually lived out. The God who was worshiped here was the God of all the earth, but access to God was strictly limited by the qualifications or lack thereof shared by the worshipers.

In Acts 8, the Ethiopian eunuch who is returning from Jerusalem to his home made that long trip to stand in prayer in the Court of the Gentiles. The next level of access was the Court of the Women, which might more accurately be called the Court of the Ritually Pure Jewish Women. Gentile women were not permitted inside the court, nor were women who were menstruating, had recently had sexual intercourse or given birth, had touched a dead body, or who had any mental or physical defect. Assuming they met all these qualifications, ritually pure Jewish women could come this far but no farther.

Beyond the Court of the Women was the Court of Israel, which might be more accurately called the Court of the Ritually Pure Jewish Men. Gentile men were not permitted here, nor were Jewish men who had touched a menstruating woman or a woman who had recently given birth, or who had had recent sexual intercourse or touched a dead body. No man with a mental or physical defect could be admitted, either. Jewish men who met all these restrictions could come into this courtyard but not into the temple itself.

Within the temple itself was a large room called the Holy or the Sanctuary. Here priests and Levites who were ritually pure could enter and offer music, prayer, and incense. Beyond an immense curtain at the rear of the Holy was the Holy of Holies, a room once containing the Ark of the Covenant but left empty in the rebuilding of the temple following its destruction by Babylon. It was here that the Name of the God of Israel was understood to dwell, and only one person out of all the earth had access to that room—the high priest—and only once a year, on the Day of Atonement.

The architecture of the temple delineated the bounded sets that together constituted the identity of Israel as a larger bounded set within the nations of the world. Jesus's entire public ministry challenged this system of limited access to God. Not only did he speak against the temple and chase the money changers from its courts, but in his person he redrew its map of access to God by choosing to talk to, touch, and heal Gentiles, both men and women; women with a flow of blood or accused of adultery; lepers, the dead, and those who had touched the dead; and people with any number of physical and mental defects. If the temple codes said that a person was unclean, Jesus welcomed him or her as a matter of policy. In light of this practice, his words recorded in Matthew 6:6 take on a revolutionary quality: "Whenever you pray, go into your room and shut the door and pray to your Father who is in secret; and your Father who sees in secret will reward you." Jesus taught those without access to the temple that access to God was theirs nonetheless. The public ministry of Jesus is nuanced differently by each of the four gospels but is consistently portrayed as restoring agency to those who depended on government and religion to take care of them.

A long history of reading the New Testament with a bias against Israel has made many preachers far too comfortable with a simplistic formula of Israel/old/bad versus Christian/new/good. Unfortunately, the history of the Christian church subsequent to the New Testament period invalidates this common framework of interpretation. The church recreated the physical architecture of the temple in its own houses of worship, separating clergy from laity with an altar rail instead of a curtain, and came up with many long lists of who is acceptable to God and who is not, who has access to God and who does not. Leadership quickly became hierarchical and top-down, and approval by God was once again based on the worth of the person rather than on the generosity of God. In spite of the New Testament's extended arguments that Jesus represented the end of sacrifice, the relationship between human beings and God was held to be mediated through a new ritual recreating the sacrifice of Jesus. The effect of all these choices was to rob the community of believers of the agency Jesus tried to restore to them, the ability to choose the reign of God for themselves and to make responsible decisions based on that allegiance in all aspects of their lives. The history of church reformations great and small in the past twenty centuries might be viewed through the lens of repeated attempts to restore agency to the believer, yet again and again Christians show their preference for a system of religious belief that invests agency in some while depriving most people of its privileges and responsibilities.

Perhaps it was inevitable that the centered set formed by Jesus—people who responded with joy to the announcement of the reign of God on earth and were prepared to reorder their lives accordingly—should become the bounded set of a new institutional religion. Yet we find seeds of a different kind of faith community in the way Jesus called his disciples and the way the first Christian communities formed themselves. If we assume that Jesus was founding a religion, we will tend to read his choice of twelve disciples as the beginning of a new organization with a board of directors. In this light, he seems to be creating a new bounded set with appointed leaders and rules. If we continue down this logical road, the fact that the twelve disciples mentioned in the New Testament were all male becomes a foundation for the argument that maleness is intrinsic to the leadership of institutional Christianity. But if we look at Jesus's choices from a social and cultural point of view, we see what a remarkable cross-section of Jewish life the twelve men Jesus gathered around him represented: from religious revolutionaries to tax-collecting collaborators, from Galilean fishers and farmers to Hellenized laborers and even Jesus's own family members. While they are often popularly portrayed as twelve illiterate fishermen, the scriptural record portrays the disciples as a far more diverse group of people who would not normally sit down to eat together. The work of proclaiming the reign of God had made of them a centered set with a common purpose. The Johannine Jesus, more of an equal-opportunity employer than his synoptic counterparts, broadens the group even further, using his linguistic fishing rod to catch men and women alike. The Samaritan woman at the well (John 4) is a textbook case of the movement from bounded to centered set: on the basis of race, culture, religion, and gender, she and Jesus should not be connecting as they do, but their conversation dissolves all these barriers and makes of the woman a Johannine missional preacher.

This boundary-crossing heterogeneity characterized early Christian communities as well. As historian Peter Brown writes in *The World of Late Antiquity*:

> In an age when the barriers separating the successful freedman from the *déclassé* senator were increasingly unreal, a religious group could take the final step of ignoring them. In Rome the Christian community of the early third century was a place where just such anomalies were gathered and tolerated: the Church included a powerful freedman chamberlain of the emperor; its bishop was the former slave of that freedman; it was protected by the emperor's mistress, and patronized by noble ladies. For [people] whose confusions came partly from feeling no longer embedded in their home environment, the Christian Church offered a drastic experiment in social living, reinforced by the excitements and occasional perils of a break with one's past and one's neighbours.[7]

Even without Brown's vivid description we see the remarkable diversity of the communities to whom Paul addresses his letters:

> I commend to you our sister Phoebe, a deacon of the church at Cenchreae . . . for she has been a benefactor of many and of myself as well. Greet Prisca and Aquila, who work with me in

Christ Jesus, and who risked their necks for my life, to whom not only I give thanks, but also all the churches of the Gentiles. Greet my beloved Epaenetus, who was the first convert in Asia for Christ. Greet Mary, who has worked very hard among you. Greet Andronicus and Junia, my relatives who were in prison with me; they are prominent among the apostles, and they were in Christ before I was. Greet Ampliatus, my beloved in the Lord. Greet Urbanus, our co-worker in Christ, and my beloved Stachys. Greet Apelles, who is approved in Christ. Greet those who belong to the family of Aristobulus. Greet my relative Herodion. Greet those in the Lord who belong to the family of Narcissus. Greet those workers in the Lord, Tryphaena and Tryphosa. Greet the beloved Persis, who has worked hard in the Lord. Greet Rufus, chosen in the Lord; and greet his mother—a mother to me also. Greet Asyncritus, Phlegon, Hermes, Patrobas, Hermas, and the brothers and sisters who are with them. Greet Philologus, Julia, Nereus and his sister, and Olympas, and all the saints who are with them.

Timothy, my co-worker, greets you; so do Lucius and Jason and Sosipater, my relatives. Gaius, who is host to me and to the whole church, greets you. Erastus, the city treasurer, and our brother Quartus, greet you.

Romans 16:1-15, 21, 23

There is no longer Jew or Greek, there is no longer slave or free, there is no longer male or female; for all of you are one in Christ Jesus.

Galations 3:28

In many ways the experience of North American Christians today has come full circle to that of people living in the New Testament period. After a long period of deliberately establishing homogenous congregations that reflected their socioeconomic surroundings, churches in Canada and the United States are being forced to adopt new practices of congregational development and create heterogenous communities that resemble those to whom Paul wrote. Changing patterns of immigration and employment have dramatically increased the diversity of many North American congregations, a phenomenon the church-growth literature of the 1980s seemed not to anticipate. But it would be naive to create a one-to-one correspondence between Paul's world and ours. The years from the end of the New Testament period to the middle of the twentieth century saw the advent of Christendom, a notion linking the gospel with manifest destiny. A key assumption of Christendom is that Christian theology provides the correct framework for interpreting all human experience. Even today we continue to call those who don't know or believe in that theology "the unchurched," as though church membership were still normative. With so many years of a Christendom mindset preceding them, preachers do not automatically feel the rush of the new that permeates the letters of Paul when they get into their pulpits. Although they have many of the same opportunities to connect with a multicultural, syncretistic audience that the preachers of the first century had, the academic discipline that prepares them for their task continues to lag behind, still teaching its students to inform and persuade, now with an even heavier emphasis on persuading.

Let's make a choice to view the glass as half full, to see the collapse of Christian empire in the West as a good thing for the church. What does all this bounded- and centered-set business mean for preaching in the twenty-first century? It seems to me that we can take pages from both Jesus and Paul and put our energy into helping both nominal and committed members of Christian congregations begin thinking of themselves as a centered set, a group of people attracted to and motivated by the announcement of the reign of God, rather than as a bounded set, the people who have their names on the books at First Church. Our first movement in that direction might be to propose a new activity for people to get involved with, creating a centered set of "the people who are committed to this project." However, preacher-proposed projects are still part of the Christendom mindset in which a few have agency and the many respond to it. Such projects still require doing things *for* instead of *as* the church, and therefore continue to shore up a maintenance mentality. But allowing congregations to choose the reign of God for themselves might have unexpected consequences outside the control of the preacher. Are we ready for that? And how might we do it, anyway?

What's in a Name? Maybe a Lot

Reformers of every stripe place a great deal of weight on the importance of language, believing that changed speech leads to changed
people. The Protestant reformers of sixteenth-century Europe in-
sisted that what had been the Mass would now become the Lord's
Supper; and the pope, no longer recognized as the head of the universal church, was demoted to being called the bishop of Rome (at
least, by those who wished to sound respectful). The first thirteen
British colonies in the New World renamed themselves the United
States of America, and post-Revolutionary Russians spoke their
new reality by calling one another "comrade." Whether a change
in language precipitates a change in practice or merely codifies
changes that have already taken place is an open question. What's
certain is that the language change itself cannot guarantee the effectiveness or longevity of the change it signals.

That being said, it can be revelatory to revisit language we take
for granted and see, perhaps for the first time, the assumptions of
thought and practice from another era encoded there. I can't remember a time when I didn't know the phrase "mad as a hatter,"
no doubt because of Lewis Carroll's *Alice in Wonderland*. But the
Mad Hatter was Lewis's fictional embodiment of a phrase already
current in his day, one he probably knew the actual derivation of.
In the nineteenth century beaver fur was a popular material for
hats, but because of its expense, cheaper furs like rabbit were frequently used as substitutes. The process of turning these cheaper
furs into a felt material suitable for making hats involved a variety
of chemical compounds that relied on mercury, and the exposure
to mercury in cramped, unventilated hat factories led to multiple
physical and mental illnesses for the workers. Dementia brought
on by overexposure to mercury in this industry came to be known
as "mad hatter syndrome." So, while twenty-first-century speakers
may use the phrase "mad as a hatter" innocently, believing they
are making a reference to a late-nineteenth-century fantasy character, the words actually carry with them a history of human suffering and exploitation. Since the kinds of labor practices embedded
in that phrase are not only widespread in the world today but on

the rise, knowing something of the history enshrined in our language can raise the awareness of North Americans about the way their lifestyle continues to be supported by the invisible suffering of many who produce attractive consumer goods.

A more contemporary example might be the changing language we use to describe physical disabilities. My own mother walked with canes when I was born, progressing to a walker and a wheelchair as her ability to get around lessened throughout her life. When I was a child in the 1960s, pretty much everyone would have said that my mother was "crippled." Crippled morphed into "handicapped" and then "disabled" during the 1960s and 1970s, then turned positive (or euphemistic) with "differently abled" in the 1980s. Around the time the Americans with Disabilities Act (ADA) became law in 1990, we began to hear the language of "physically challenged." I continue to favor this language, because it seems an accurate description of my mother's experience and conveys neither pity nor false cheer. But it seems not to have caught on, perhaps because of its overuse in often comic ways ("Interior Design for the Color-Challenged" came up on an Internet search). But behind all the changes in language was a quest for agency, a goal made marvelously possible by the ADA. For most of her life, my mother couldn't participate in many activities outside her home because of the countless obstacles the world presented her: getting through a door, or up a flight of stairs, or into and out of a bathroom stall. When she did attempt to meet these challenges, she often had to become completely dependent on others, relying on strong arms to lift her chair up a non-negotiable flight of two steps, or on a sympathetic stranger to help her onto and off a toilet once she'd managed to get as far as the stall. She found these experiences so humiliating that she preferred to stay at home. The ADA wasn't about sympathy but agency, allowing men, women, and children with a host of challenges to meet those challenges by themselves.

It might be helpful to think of missional preaching as the ADA for congregations. A lot of this book has been about acts of imagination, and the ADA itself began as a reimagining of what life might be like for people who had lost or never had all the agency granted to people with sight, hearing, and arms and legs that

worked reasonably well. One way to help the congregation reimagine itself and its agency is to examine some of the language of
the church's life that we no longer think about because its origins
are so distant.

Sheep and Shepherds

The word "congregation" is a Latinate word built from the root
"grex/gregis," or "sheep." A con-greg-ation is a gathering of sheep,
or a flock. No real surprises there, given that the English word
"flock" is commonly used to describe the Christian community
gathered. And rare indeed is the "congregant" who has not heard
one or more sermons about the negative qualities of sheep—how
they are dirty, stupid, and completely dependent—a message that
has always seemed deeply hostile to me but that seems to be met
with cheerful laughter wherever it is preached. The metaphor is so
entrenched that "pastor," Latin for "shepherd," has become syn-
onymous with "clergy" in virtually all Christian denominations.
Indeed, "pastor" is currently resurgent in denominations that
formerly used more idiosyncratic titles, since the church-growth
movement of the 1980s began to stress accessibility to seekers.
"Pastor" is a word people recognize, and a multitude of associations and assumptions go along with it, even for the minimally
churched. We cannot overestimate the comfort factor in joining
a "flock" watched over by a "shepherd" who has closer access to
God and who will see to our needs for security and meaning in an
increasingly meaningless and violent world.

While the image of shepherd does occur in the New Testament,
it most often describes Jesus. The community of faith gathered is
more often described as the "assembly" (*ekklesia*), a word that has
its root not in "sheep" but in "call." *Kaleo* is the verb "to call"
in Greek, and those who are "called out" (*ek-kaleo*) form the assembly. The word had clear political connotations in the Graeco-
Roman empire, as it did at the time of the writing of the United
States Constitution, when the "right of the people peaceably to
assemble" was guaranteed by the First Amendment. The fact that
"assemblies" have power to effect change may well explain why

this right is not universally guaranteed throughout the globe, nor fully appreciated by the country that put it in writing two centuries ago. The Second Vatican Council invoked the ancient name of the assembly in an attempt to reinvigorate participation in Roman Catholic worship, and other denominations that were affected by the liturgical renewal of the last half of the twentieth century followed suit. The use of "assembly" in place of "congregation" is widespread in the Roman Catholic Church today, somewhat common in the Anglican and Lutheran Churches, and used by seminary professors of worship of many Protestant denominations. But like the phrase "physically challenged," it has not caught on universally, perhaps for similar reasons. The words "physically challenged" tell us something about the world we have created, full of obstacles for people who have difficulty navigating those obstacles through no fault of their own. It makes us think about what needs to be done to restore equity. Just so, calling the gathered body of Christians "the assembly" has implications for the kind of internal world the church has created, a world in which laypeople have been characterized as sheep for generations. If the sheep decide they have agency, they may cause problems. The shepherd will have to go off looking for them, or untangle them from a bush, or prevent them from drinking contaminated water. Sheep need to follow the guidance of their shepherd for the whole system to work. Warren hits the nail on the head when he writes:

> Naming the gathering for worship an "assembly" does not produce the reality signified by this word, though it does problematize what happens during that gathering. Restoring in any deep way the political dimensions of how we come together calls for more than updated liturgical choreography; it will involve fundamental changes in the way each person conceives of the self as an agent in an agent-full assembly. For a community this self-understanding will not come from being preached to about agency but from transformation in the way people come together and act in their togetherness.[8]

Because he is writing about "how we speak in the church" in this chapter and about preaching as a subset of that speaking,

Warren goes on to suggest a way of restoring the agency that the captive-audience aspect of listening to a sermon robs listeners of: distributing the lessons for the coming Sunday the week before, allowing people to read and pray with them, and then to gather in small groups to share their responses to the Word of God when the assembly gathers on Sunday. This method has been developed pretty fully by the work of John McClure (*The Roundtable Pulpit*) and Lucy Atkinson Rose (*Sharing the Word: Preaching in the Roundtable Church*).[9] I have participated in services where the practice is employed, and I've offered it to parishes I've served. I think it can be effective as a first step away from passivity around the interpretation of Scripture. But I also believe it represents a rather limited vision of the way the reign of God can continue to empower the imaginations of men and women today. While it appears to decentralize the power to interpret Scripture, it continues to be clergy-driven because of the disparity in the knowledge of Scripture and academic theology between the ordained and the non-ordained. Missional preaching needs to do more to place the choice for the reign of God before listeners. It must restore that sense of "crisis" discussed in the first and third chapters of this book. Only when the gathered assembly can discern the implications of choosing the reign of God for itself has the preacher truly gotten out of the way. That shared discernment, in turn, can lead both preacher and assembly to embrace an apostolic identity in the world and ask, "What is this assembly sent to do in the world? How do our different roles support the choices we have made?"

The parish I described in the second chapter, where the little girl holding up the ciborium made me question my whole preaching ministry, had ongoing conversation about all these topics over a period of months and years. We talked not only about the difference between being a congregation and an assembly but also about other shifts in language coming out of the post–Second World War liturgical renewal, like the recognition that it is the members of the assembly, not the priest, who celebrate the Eucharist. This recognition has led to the substitution of "presider" (someone who "sits in front," somewhat confusingly styled as "president" in English-speaking churches following the British usage) for "celebrant." Those conversations inspired the lay leaders of the congregation to write an identity statement that we used in the bulletin and newsletter and on the parish Web site:

> We are the assembly, the people called out by our baptisms to proclaim God's reign of love and justice breaking into a world of hate and injustice. Together, we make eucharist, blessing and eating bread and wine as Jesus commanded us in order to be strengthened by his living presence for our own lives of Christian witness. Everyone present today is a celebrant of the eucharist; our worship is led by lay and ordained presiders.

When I show this paragraph to seminarians and clergy, it meets with decidedly mixed reactions. Most assume that I wrote it myself without any consultation with the parishioners; that is not, in fact, the case, but the assumption is revealing. Others remark on the lack of denominational identity and information about how to participate in worship or to get involved with the church. Some are inspired by it. Some find it "too political." But everyone recognizes that it does offer a clear vision of a kind of organization very different from those most seminarians and clergy have been prepared to lead. To the extent that these words might become self-implicating, a standard against which we measure our shared life, they were and are the template for being a different kind of Christian community. We were moving from being a bounded set (the Episcopal Church in this suburb) to a centered set (the people called and sent by their baptism from this house of worship into the world). I didn't have the language during the seven years I served that parish, but today I would say that together our imaginations became seized by a longing for the reign of God to come among us in ways we could name in our personal and public lives.

And so we come to another layer of the onion of missional preaching: To address the gathered Christian body week in and week out as an assembly—as people who might freely choose the reign of God proclaimed in their hearing—preachers will have to read the Bible missionally as well. We will need to stop reading it as a closed book of ancient stories and fixed rules and start reading it as a testimony to the missional God whose activity continues to this moment.

CHAPTER 6

Reimagining Scripture

The title of this chapter may suggest that I've gone too far. Imagination in preaching is generally considered a good thing, but an imaginative approach to the Bible raises the red flag of *eisegesis*, or reading into the Bible more than it actually says. My intention in this chapter, however, is to reimagine not the *content* of Scripture but the *framework of interpretation* we bring to it. This interpretive framework is the result of two millennia of institutional Christianity during which the Bible came to be viewed as a closed canon. The polarizing approaches to Scripture that preoccupied the twentieth century—the Bible as timeless Word of God or time-bound record of the beliefs of ancient peoples—have tended to become even more entrenched in the twenty-first. What began as a debate among nineteenth-century European scholars has long since led to the separation of whole denominations from one another and splintered those bodies internally. The kind of reimagining this chapter will talk about does not require a choice between these divided camps fighting over how literally to take the Bible, but it can work equally well for interpreters who place themselves anywhere on that spectrum. The kind of reimagining this chapter will discuss uses the internal logic of the Bible itself to reclaim its orientation toward God's future.

Missional preaching can't simply be a matter of announcing the reign of God come among us and demanding that listeners choose it week after week. That would get old in about a month.

Instead, missional preaching requires us to support our rekindled vision of the kingdom of God and our renewed sense of the congregation's agency with a habitual approach to reading the Bible that discovers in it the *missionality of God*. The fundamental question becomes whether we believe that the activity of God in human history is functionally complete or that it continues in the present. Naturally, every Christian preacher would say that God is alive, well, and active in the present moment; yet most tend to approach the Bible in a way that contradicts this stated belief. No matter what seminary preachers attended, some version of "salvation history" was presented to them as the framework for interpreting the Bible. Salvation history is a kind of script of God's plan that, like a good screenplay, leads to a satisfying conclusion. I certainly don't intend to argue against the notion of a history of salvation; I'd have to give up my Christian faith to do that. But I do want to argue that the verb tenses we use when we talk about that history make a mountain of difference.

To the extent that salvation history is the story of what God *did*, it is a story of the past. All that's left to do is to tell people that story—and soon we find ourselves back to informing and persuading! Another possibility is to view the story of the Bible as continuing into the present, changing all the verbs to the present tense. Such a hermeneutical move is not intended to reduce the historical claims of the Bible to mere symbolic patterns; rather, it is a renewed acknowledgment that we are living today *in the midst of* the timeline described by the Bible's trajectory, which begins in prehistory and looks ahead to post-history, the New Jerusalem. The Revelation to John points to a goal not yet realized, so the framers of the canon placed us squarely in the middle of what came to be known as "salvation history." Because of the stunning success of Christianity as an institutional religion, the urgent sense of God's imminent action that pervades the New Testament was discarded. In its place the church created a kind of "CliffsNotes" version of the scriptural story that could be presented easily to people who had never heard it. In fact, the impetus for creating a canon at all was the impulse to market the Christian story more effectively, and the invention of the codex—a book with a spine to replace a cabinet full of scrolls—at that very moment in history helped to shape the story of salvation in a definitive way. Unlike a scroll, a codex has a beginning, middle, and end, and it is read in one direction. We cannot overestimate the effect this innovation had on what became the Christian view of the history of the world. As the church swelled its numbers and gained earthly power while the numbers and power of the Roman Empire collapsed, it had less need for an eschatological intervention to justify the saints. So, in the same way that the kingdom of God came to mean the place we go when we die or the growth of the visible church in contradiction to its meaning in the gospels, the Bible became the story of What God Did. It now had a beginning, middle, and end, and it no longer testified to the continuing missional nature of God. Arranged as an outline it would look like this:

Salvation History as Completed

God created the world.
God created the human race.
The human race fell into sin.
God created Israel to redeem the human race.
God sent the prophets to remind Israel of its calling and prepare for the salvation of all humanity.
God sent Jesus to redeem the human race from sin by dying on the cross.
God sent the Holy Spirit to call the church into being and lead it into all truth.
Mission accomplished.

A missional reading of this same story would take seriously that we are still in the midst of the outline of salvation presented in Scripture and would emphasize the present nature of God's continual sending. Some words from David Bosch's *Transforming Mission* will contextualize this reimagining:

During the past half century or so[1] there has been a subtle but nevertheless decisive shift toward understanding mission as God's mission. During preceding centuries mission was understood in a variety of ways. Sometimes it was interpreted primarily in soteriological terms: as saving individuals from eternal damnation. Or it was understood in cultural terms: as introducing people from the East and the South to the blessings and privileges of the Christian West. Often it was perceived in ecclesiastical categories: as the expansion of the church (or of a specific denomination). Sometimes it was defined salvation-historically: as the process by which the world . . . would be transformed into the kingdom of God. After the First World War, however, missiologists began to take note of recent developments in biblical and systematic theology. In a paper read at the Brandenburg Missionary Conference in 1932, Karl Barth became one of the first theologians to articulate mission as an activity of God himself. [At the Willingen Conference in 1952] the classical doctrine of the *missio Dei* as God the Father sending the Son, and God the Father and the Son sending the Spirit was expanded to include yet another "movement": Father, Son and Holy Spirit sending the church into the world.

In the new image mission is not primarily an activity of the church, but an attribute of God. "It is not the church that has a mission of salvation to fulfill in the world; it is the mission of the Son and the Spirit through the Father that includes the church" (Moltmann, *The Church in the Power of the Spirit,* 1977:64). There is church because there is mission, not vice versa. To participate in mission is to participate in the movement of God's love toward people, since God is a fountain of sending love.[2]

When we combine this paradigm shift—the impetus for this entire book—with our developing ideas of the kingdom of God and the agency of the assembly, a missional reading of the whole of Scripture might look like this:

Salvation History as Continuing

God sends the Spirit to create the world.
The human race chooses away from God.
God sends Abraham and Sarah to create Israel and offer
    the choice again.

> God sends the prophets when Israel chooses to imitate oth-
> er patterns of power, namely salvation through a king.
> God sends Jesus to proclaim the direct reign of God
> when the hope of salvation through a human king is
> exhausted.
> God sends the Spirit to confirm Jesus's proclamation of the
> reign of God and stir up the power of God's reign in
> the gathered assembly.
> God sends the church to bear witness to the power of God's
> reign on earth and heal.
> Mission ongoing . . .

Let me say at once that there is absolutely nothing wrong with the first outline of salvation history as found in Scripture; this is not a question of "old equals bad" versus "new equals good." It is a question of reading the Bible for maintenance sermons versus reading it for missional sermons. The approach represented by the first outline, recognizable to Christians throughout the world and in most ages, is the way most clergy are taught to think about the Bible. It is not wrong, but it is guaranteed to produce maintenance sermons, because it views salvation history as completed. The approach represented by the second outline cannot of itself produce missional sermons, but it can support and inspire them. It is a way of reading Scripture that is more familiar in the synagogue, where the Torah is still read from scrolls instead of from a codex or bound book.

Nowhere does the synagogue's approach to Scripture come into sharper focus than on the festival of Simchat Torah (Hebrew, "Rejoicing with the Torah"), which concludes the Jewish liturgical year. It comes just after the seven-day festival of Sukkot, or Booths, and celebrates the completion of the one-year lectionary of readings that have taken each synagogue's assembly[3] through the entire Torah. While the most logical portion of Torah to be read on this occasion might be simply the final chapter of Deuteronomy, the last of the five Books of Moses, in fact there are two readings: Deuteronomy 33:1-34:12 (the final verses of that book) followed by Genesis 1:1-2:3, beginning the cycle of Torah readings over again practically in the same breath. The Torah scrolls are carried in procession or danced around the sanctuary or into the streets and then carefully rewound to begin the story of the creation of the world and the creation of Israel anew the coming Sabbath.

There are a number of implications to this practice. Theologically, it joins the story of Israel camped at Jordan and waiting to inherit the Promised Land to the power of God to create everything out of nothing. This linkage is particularly poignant in light of the disappointments that Israel experienced during the biblical period and subsequently. It says that when God's promises seem to have failed, the creative power of God is always able to begin again. God is always creating and recreating Israel. As a physical symbol, the rewinding of the Torah scroll makes of the stories contained therein an ever-present loop without beginning or end but perpetually interpretable by new generations. The agency of Jews in relation to their Scripture is dramatically evident in the ceremonies of bar and bat mitzvah, when young people around the age of fourteen are "called to the Torah" to chant the appointed portion and then offer a "d'var Torah," a word of interpretation to the assembly of those who have gathered to watch their rite of passage. It is considered essential for every member of the Jewish community to take ownership of the ancient texts of Scripture and continue their interpretation in the present.

Christians, particularly those who gain most of their exposure to the Bible by listening to sermons, could benefit from a similar approach to Scripture. Many probably share the view of the biblical story expressed by Katherine Hepburn in the movie adaptation of Jean Giraudoux's play "The Madwoman of Chaillot": "It all seems so impersonal, so long ago." I often show a clip from this film in my classes on missional preaching, because I believe it epitomizes the theological landscape into which a renewed proclamation of the reign of God must be introduced. Giraudoux's play, an allegory of the clash between ancient codes of civility and modern greed epitomized by the lust for oil, pits the "madwoman," a faded aristocrat who dresses in old age as she did when a young woman, against representatives of the interlocked powers of Western capitalism: big business, the military, politicians, and religion. The representative of religion, a Billy Graham–style evangelist played by John Gavin, hopes for a large donation from the madwoman (played by Hepburn). In this scene he tries to convince her of the truth of Christianity by giving her an outline of history that sounds very much like the outline on page 87 above:

EVANGELIST: [The Lord] sent you here for one good reason: to protect you. You know that, don't you?

MADWOMAN: What am I being protected *from*?

EVANGELIST: You heard me out there tonight, calling on all those sinners! That city out there is just festering with sin.

MADWOMAN: I've always been somewhat confused as to the exact definition of sin.

EVANGELIST: Sin is disobedience to God. Now, we're all sinners to the extent that we were conceived and born in sin. That's God's punishment for man for defying him in the Garden of Eden. He had to send down his only Son to redeem us from it.

MADWOMAN: Yes . . . forgive me . . . it all seems such a long time ago, so impersonal, in a way . . . so *vindictive*. You don't think God might be a woman, do you?

EVANGELIST: *(Startled)* Certainly not! No, ma'am, I can assure you that God is not a woman. He created man in his own image and he forbade Adam and Eve to eat of the apple. He knew Satan would tempt them to disobey, but he was testing man to see if man would serve him or Satan.

MADWOMAN: He wasn't sure.

EVANGELIST: Well, of course he was sure! God can't be surprised.

MADWOMAN: Oh! How dull for him.

EVANGELIST: He knew Adam and Eve would eat of the apple.

MADWOMAN: But if he knew, why did he bother? That seems rather frivolous. I mean, wouldn't you agree? It's such an awful lot of trouble to go to over a personal fight with Satan. Actually, if he hadn't let them eat the apple in the first place, he needn't have sent his son.

EVANGELIST: Well, ma'am, the fact is, he did send his Son. So now there is no longer any excuse for the obstinate sinner. The path to salvation is open to every Christian.

MADWOMAN: Oh, it's limited, is it?

EVANGELIST: *(Startled)* I beg your pardon?

MADWOMAN: Limited to Christians?

EVANGELIST: Well, in a sense, yes.

MADWOMAN: What sort of sense is that?

EVANGELIST: It's very good sense! I mean, there *is* only one true religion.

MADWOMAN: Well, who decided that? Did God take care of that, too? I mean, I'm not what you'd call a much-traveled woman, but I seem to recall in some of the better-quality pictorial magazines that in some of the more out-of-the-way places God hasn't made that quite clear.

EVANGELIST: The point is, we're still trying to push God's message across.

MADWOMAN: Yes . . . seems odd he didn't do it himself. I mean, he arranged all the nasty bits so well.[4]

Despite some of the dated gender stereotypes in this exchange, it remains almost prescient about the situation facing preachers in the early twenty-first century, when secularism has become far more widespread in the Western world and the supremacy of Christianity among world religions is no longer a given, even for many Christians. Christian preachers ought to be having these exchanges all the time; if they did, they might develop better answers than John Gavin's character was able to come up with on the spur of the moment. In reality, however, clergy and seminary faculty *talk about* the secular world far more than they engage it. More often than not, that talk is about how to inform and persuade the secular world into a Christian view. The outline of the Christian faith that the evangelist recites for the madwoman is, more or less, what is offered to seminarians of every stripe as the basis for their theological education. They fill it out with more content and nuances, but the outline of "salvation history" that rolls off the evangelist's tongue can roll off the tongues of most seminary graduates and clergy as well. Its formulaic nature makes sense of the universe and offers clear moral choices. And, of course, it can all be backed up by Scripture. That is, one or more scriptural texts can be *found* to back up the evangelist's outline or the chart on page 87 above, "Salvation History as Completed." But few seem to notice (or want to admit) that what emerges from this process is a kind of tautology: we find this story in Scripture because we use it as our lens for reading it. That doesn't make it wrong, but it does contextualize and historicize our reading. The outline of salvation history based on human failure and divine redemption has proved a highly successful marketing tool for millennia, perhaps most of all because it makes the Bible *all about us*. But as any regular reader of the Bible knows, seminary-trained or simply faithful, the Bible is at least as much *about God* as it is about us, and the God of the Bible is a missional God, a God whose very nature is *to send*. Read through the lens of missionality, the Bible is not a story about what God *did* but about what God *does*, a revelation of the possibilities inherent in the present moment rather than a body of information about the past.

So how might we engage in a missional reading of the Bible? The first thing to realize is that we won't be doing something new, but something ancient, embracing a way of thinking about salvation history that is evidenced in countless places in the Bible itself. To do this reading, we *will* be throwing off the legacy of Christendom, with its assumption that salvation history is complete and neatly packaged for distribution, but we will by no means be trying to imagine a "new" Bible. "It all seems such a long time ago, so impersonal," the madwoman of Chaillot says. But this was not the way the Scriptures were read by Jesus or by those he first sent to proclaim the kingdom of God and to heal. The first missional preachers, like their predecessors in the biblical narrative, believed that everything the Scriptures pointed to was coming to pass, and that they were the next chapter in the scriptural story.

Proclamation and Agency in the Scriptural Narrative

Using the building blocks of our developing paradigm, we can look at Scripture and see that inviting a whole community to choose the reign of God did not begin with Jesus and his sent preachers. Out of a plethora of choices I've selected four key moments from the biblical story to show that missional preaching is more ancient than it is new. The first comes from the moment in the Book of Joshua when Joshua has assumed leadership of the community of Israel as the people prepare to cross the Jordan into the Promised Land.

> Then Joshua gathered all the tribes of Israel to Shechem, and summoned the elders, the heads, the judges, and the officers of Israel; and they presented themselves before God. And Joshua said to all the people, "Thus says the LORD, the God of Israel: Long ago your ancestors—Terah and his sons Abraham and Na- hor—lived beyond the Euphrates and served other gods. Then I took your father Abraham from beyond the River and led him through all the land of Canaan and made his offspring many. I gave him Isaac; and to Isaac I gave Jacob and Esau. I gave Esau the hill country of Seir to possess, but Jacob and his chil- dren went down to Egypt. Then I sent Moses and Aaron, and I plagued Egypt with what I did in its midst; and afterwards I brought you out. When I brought your ancestors out of Egypt, you came to the sea; and the Egyptians pursued your ancestors with chariots and horsemen to the Red Sea. When they cried out to the LORD, he put darkness between you and the Egyptians, and made the sea come upon them and cover them; and your eyes saw what I did to Egypt. Afterwards you lived in the wilder- ness a long time. Then I brought you to the land of the Amorites, who lived on the other side of the Jordan; they fought with you, and I handed them over to you, and you took possession of their land, and I destroyed them before you. Then King Balak son of Zippor of Moab, set out to fight against Israel. He sent and invited Balaam son of Beor to curse you, but I would not listen to Balaam; therefore he blessed you; so I rescued you out of his hand. When you went over the Jordan and came to Jericho, the citizens of Jericho fought against you, and also the Amorites, the Perizzites, the Canaanites, the Hittites, the Girgashites, the Hiv- ites, and the Jebusites; and I handed them over to you. I sent the hornet ahead of you, which drove out before you the two kings

of the Amorites; it was not by your sword or by your bow. I gave you a land on which you had not labored, and towns that you had not built, and you live in them; you eat the fruit of vineyards and oliveyards that you did not plant.

"Now therefore revere the LORD, and serve him in sincerity and in faithfulness; put away the gods that your ancestors served beyond the River and in Egypt, and serve the LORD. Now if you are unwilling to serve the LORD, choose this day whom you will serve, whether the gods your ancestors served in the region beyond the River or the gods of the Amorites in whose land you are living; but as for me and my household, we will serve the LORD."

Then the people answered, "Far be it from us that we should forsake the LORD to serve other gods; for it is the LORD our God who brought us and our ancestors up from the land of Egypt, out of the house of slavery, and who did those great signs in our sight. He protected us along all the way that we went, and among all the peoples through whom we passed; and the Lord drove out before us all the peoples, the Amorites who lived in the land. Therefore we also will serve the LORD, for he is our God."

But Joshua said to the people, "You cannot serve the LORD, for he is a holy God. He is a jealous God; he will not forgive your transgressions or your sins. If you forsake the LORD and serve foreign gods, then he will turn and do you harm, and consume you, after having done you good." And the people said to Joshua, "No, we will serve the LORD!" Then Joshua said to the people, "You are witnesses against yourselves that you have chosen the LORD, to serve him." And they said, "We are witnesses." He said, "Then put away the foreign gods that are among you, and incline your hearts to the LORD, the God of Israel." The people said to Joshua, "The LORD our God we will serve, and him we will obey."

Joshua 24:1-24

Notice some of the key elements of this speech. Joshua begins with a retelling of the history of God's actions with Israel to date. But this is not a catechism to be memorized by adolescents; it's a recontextualizing of the present moment, implying that all that

ancient history—far from being impersonal—leads right up to the
present and now requires a response by people who are alive and
breathing and listening to Joshua speak. The second thing to notice is that Joshua doesn't simply tell the people how they need
to respond: he asks them to make a choice and even pushes them
after their first "correct" answer to be sure they understand the
costs as well as the benefits of their free choice.

A second forerunner of missional preaching comes from the
other side of Israel's experience with the Promised Land, at the
very moment when it is being lost. The prophet Jeremiah writes
to the cream of Israelite society—its royal family and its court, its
religious leaders and scholars, its artists and artisans—all of whom
have been taken by King Nebuchadnezzar to live in exile in Babylon. Jeremiah offers a theological interpretation of the devastating
experience the community is living through and asks them to make
choices about their future in light of that interpretation.

> These are the words of the letter that the prophet Jeremiah sent
> from Jerusalem to the remaining elders among the exiles, and to
> the priests, the prophets, and all the people, whom Nebuchad-
> nezzar had taken into exile from Jerusalem to Babylon. This was
> after King Jeconiah, and the queen mother, the court officials,
> the leaders of Judah and Jerusalem, the artisans, and the smiths
> had departed from Jerusalem. The letter was sent by the hand
> of Elasah son of Shaphan and Gemariah son of Hilkiah, whom
> King Zedekiah of Judah sent to Babylon to King Nebuchadnez-
> zar of Babylon. It said: Thus says the LORD of hosts, the God of
> Israel, to all the exiles whom I have sent into exile from Jerusa-
> lem to Babylon: Build houses and live in them; plant gardens and
> eat what they produce. Take wives and have sons and daughters;
> take wives for your sons, and give your daughters in marriage,
> that they may bear sons and daughters; multiply there, and do
> not decrease. But seek the welfare of the city where I have sent
> you into exile, and pray to the LORD on its behalf, for in its wel-
> fare you will find your welfare. For thus says the LORD of hosts,
> the God of Israel: Do not let the prophets and the diviners who
> are among you deceive you, and do not listen to the dreams that
> they dream, for it is a lie that they are prophesying to you in

my name; I did not send them, says the LORD. For thus says the
LORD: Only when Babylon's seventy years are completed will I
visit you, and I will fulfill to you my promise and bring you back
to this place. For surely I know the plans I have for you, says
the LORD, plans for your welfare and not for harm, to give you
a future with hope. Then when you call upon me and come and
pray to me, I will hear you. When you search for me, you will
find me; if you seek me with all your heart, I will let you find me,
says the LORD, and I will restore your fortunes and gather you
from all the nations and all the places where I have driven you,
says the LORD, and I will bring you back to the place from which
I sent you into exile.

Jeremiah 29:1-14

The twenty-ninth chapter of Jeremiah portrays a vivid moment of *crisis* in both senses of the word for the community of
Israel divided by exile. The people are undergoing the devastation
of military defeat and occupation, and they must also discern the
theological meaning of history without the benefit of hindsight.
Shemaiah, a prophet with the exiled community, fires back a response to Jeremiah's letter expressing outrage that the remnant of
the temple leadership has not arrested Jeremiah for his blasphemy:
"Why have you not rebuked Jeremiah of Anathoth who plays the
prophet for you? For he has actually sent to us in Babylon, saying,
'It will be a long time; build houses . . . '" (vv. 27-28). Jeremiah in
turn predicts a dire end for Shemaiah and his descendants, proph-
esying that they will not live to see God's restoration of the exiles
(vv. 30-32).

People who experience defeat in warfare, from ancient Troy to
the citizens of the United States after the attacks of September 11,
2001, perennially struggle to discern the presence of God in the
midst of their calamities. The problem was particularly acute for
Israel because of its long tradition of interpreting its history along
a consistent theological trajectory. Of course, that theology of con-
quest, loss, and restoration based on faithfulness or unfaithfulness
to the Mosaic covenant received its final shape by the Scriptures'
final redactors, but their interpretation was not imposed on a *ta-
bula rasa* of otherwise secular history. Israel consistently organized

its public life around God's will and promises as touchstones, even when that still center only made the people's straying from it more obvious. Now the exiles in Babylon were faced with a particularly difficult moment of theological interpretation. Deprived of every familiar anchor, they had only written words to offer them hope for living under God's reign on foreign soil. A recognized prophet in their own midst—a resident chaplain, as it were—urges them to disregard the written words as false. What Jeremiah tells them to do—to live *as if* God were about to redeem them—must surely have seemed counterintuitive at best and repugnant at worst. The book of the prophet Jeremiah does not record the personal responses of the exiled community, but we can nevertheless draw some significant conclusions from the content of the prophet's address to them.

Through the address of the prophet, the exiles, seemingly robbed of agency, have the chance to reclaim their spiritual birthright and to live daily in the confidence of God's promise of restoration—a promise renewed by Jeremiah's letter. Everyday life in captivity can thus be shaped by the free choice of individuals and a whole community to treat human words as the revelation of a divine and trustworthy truth. We cannot know the details of that daily life, but the fact that the writings of the prophet Jeremiah are now enshrined in Scripture while the name of Shemaiah has become an obscure footnote surely testifies to the efficacy of his "preaching."

A third example of speech that proclaims the present reality of God's action and encourages agency in response to it comes from the period of the return from exile, spanning the years from 538 to 444 BCE. This passage is read by churches using either the Common Lectionary or the Revised Common Lectionary on the Third Sunday after Epiphany, Year C. The twofold efforts to rebuild the city of Jerusalem and the temple physically and to rebuild the people of Israel spiritually go hand in hand in the books of Ezra and Nehemiah. Here the governor (Nehemiah) and the chief priest and teacher of the Law (Ezra) are portrayed instructing the assembly of Israel in a tradition and language that had been nearly forgotten.

All the people gathered together into the square before the Water Gate. They told the scribe Ezra to bring the book of the law of Moses, which the LORD had given to Israel. Accordingly, the priest Ezra brought the law before the assembly, both men and women and all who could hear with understanding. This was on the first day of the seventh month. He read from it facing the square before the Water Gate from early morning until midday, in the presence of the men and the women and those who could understand; and the ears of all the people were attentive to the book of the law. . . . Then Ezra blessed the LORD, the great God, and all the people answered, "Amen, Amen," lifting up their hands. Then they bowed their heads and worshiped the LORD with their faces to the ground. . . . So they read from the book, from the law of God, with interpretation. They gave the sense, so that the people understood the reading.

And Nehemiah, who was the governor, and Ezra the priest and scribe, and the Levites who taught the people said to all the people, "This day is holy to the LORD your God; do not mourn or weep." For all the people wept when they heard the words of the law. Then he said to them, "Go your way, eat the fat and drink sweet wine and send portions of them to those for whom nothing is prepared, for this day is holy to our LORD; and do not be grieved, for the joy of the LORD is your strength." So the Levites stilled all the people, saying, "Be quiet, for this day is holy; do not be grieved." And all the people went their way to eat and drink and to send portions and to make great rejoicing, because they had understood the words that were declared to them.

Nehemiah 8:1-12 (4-5, 7 omitted)

This dramatic and moving story highlights the potential cost of choosing the reign of God, a cost that Joshua warned of in our first example above. After the devastation and disarray of the exile and its aftermath, Jerusalem and Judah might have been forgiven if they'd opted for the path of least resistance, leaving the walls of Jerusalem in rubble and going through the motions of religious observance with a shoddily thrown-together parody of the former temple's glory. But the words of Ezra and Nehemiah reconnect them to their spiritual heritage and reawaken the possibility of being and doing more. "The book of the law of Moses" remains unidentified, but we can assume that the readings are in Hebrew and the interpretations in Aramaic, the now more-familiar language of the blended community of those who returned from exile and those who never left the land. What had seemed "such a long time ago, so impersonal" suddenly becomes another moment of *crisis* for the community of faith, a keen sense of falling short of the glory of God, along with a discernment that it might have been otherwise; hence the tears of lamentation and regret. Or perhaps, more accurately, they are tears of recognition, as a new generation rediscovers its deepest identity in the religious tradition it had nearly forgotten. The words of interpretation offered by Ezra, Nehemiah, and the Levites not only reconnect the assembly with the mission of God in history, they also suggest *practices* for the coming days that reinforce this missional theology and allow listeners to remind themselves of what scriptural history has to do with them: "Eat the fat and drink sweet wine and send portions to those for whom nothing is prepared . . ."

The final paradigm for missional preaching within the Scripture itself is what's often described as the "inaugural sermon" of Jesus at Nazareth, but if it's a sermon, it's more in the model of our previous example from Nehemiah, an act of interpreting the Scriptures in a way that brings their story right into the present moment. And it's paired with the Nehemiah passage on the Third Sunday after Epiphany, Year C, in both the Common and Revised Common Lectionaries. Jesus has just completed his period of fasting and temptation in the wilderness and chooses the synagogue in his hometown to launch his public ministry. Initially well received, Jesus goes on to offer a bit more interpretation of Scripture that leads to a violent reaction.

> Then Jesus, filled with the power of the Spirit, returned to Galilee, and a report about him spread through all the surrounding country. He began to teach in their synagogues and was praised by everyone.
>
> When he came to Nazareth, where he had been brought up, he went to the synagogue on the sabbath day, as was his custom. He stood up to read, and the scroll of the prophet Isaiah was given to him. He unrolled the scroll and found the place where it was written:

"The Spirit of the Lord is upon me,
because he has anointed me to bring good news to the
    poor.
He has sent me to proclaim release to the captives
and recovery of sight to the blind,
to let the oppressed go free,
to proclaim the year of the Lord's favor."

And he rolled up the scroll, gave it back to the attendant, and sat down. The eyes of all in the synagogue were fixed on him. Then he began to say to them, "Today this scripture has been fulfilled in your hearing." All spoke well of him and were amazed at the gracious words that came from his mouth. They said, "Is not this Joseph's son?" He said to them, "Doubtless you will quote to me this proverb, 'Doctor, cure yourself!' And you will say, 'Do here also in your hometown the things that we have heard you did at Capernaum.'" And he said, "Truly I tell you, no prophet is accepted in the prophet's hometown. But the truth is, there were many widows in Israel in the time of Elijah, when the heaven was shut up three years and six months, and there was a severe famine over all the land; yet Elijah was sent to none of them except to a widow at Zarephath in Sidon. There were also many lepers in Israel in the time of the prophet Elisha, and none of them was cleansed except Naaman the Syrian." When they heard this, all in the synagogue were filled with rage. They got up, drove him out of the town, and led him to the brow of the hill on which their town was built, so that they might hurl him off the cliff. But he passed through the midst of them and went on his way.

Luke 4:14-30

Perhaps not surprisingly, given the Lukan authorship of this passage and our seminal passage in the ninth chapter of the same gospel, we find here all the hallmarks of missional preaching. Jesus identifies himself as one "sent to proclaim," he interprets scriptural history in a way that brings it right to the listeners' door, and he describes the "year of the Lord's favor" as one that has political and economic implications. So far, so good. But Jesus goes on to characterize the missionality of God as breaking all boundaries of culture and religion. Elijah was "sent" to a Gentile woman when Israel could have used his help, and a Syrian was healed of his infirmity when many Israelites remained lepers. His implication is immediately apparent to his listeners: the reign of God is for everyone who chooses it, not just for those who claim it as their divine legacy (or assume its possession by virtue of institutional membership). Of course, Luke has an agenda in this presentation of Jesus's first message; he is laying the groundwork for the rejection of Jesus by Israel and his acceptance as messiah by the Gentiles. The synagogue audience at Nazareth prefigures the teeth-gnashing crowds of the Acts of the Apostles when "the Jews" will consistently try to impede the apostolic preaching. Whatever we may think of Luke's not-so-subtle intentions, the fact is that the Lukan Jesus is calling to mind *Israel's own scriptural record.* These stories that show God's mission extending beyond the boundaries of the community of faith were already in the Scriptures for Jesus to summon up, just as the economic leveling of the Jubilee year was already enshrined in Leviticus 25. As a method of reading the Scriptures missionally, the "sermon" at Nazareth transcends Luke's indictment of the community of Israel and demonstrates a phenomenon present throughout North American Christianity today. Congregations all say they want sermons that make the Scriptures "relevant," until the "relevance" demands a response from them, perhaps even a change of behavior that goes beyond personal moral choices and involves the whole community. At such times, the madwoman's description of the scriptural story as "such a long time ago, so impersonal" may become downright attractive.

These four examples are not intended as "proof texts" for the notion of missional preaching. Rather, they reveal a deep pattern in the Bible of God's sending the offer of life under God's reign and the various human responses that sending elicits. The shape of that offer is a rehearsal of what God has done in the past in order to delineate the shape of what God is doing now, in the listeners' hearing, followed by an invitation to receive or participate in that action. It requires a community of faith convinced of its agency, one willing to use that agency to discern God's action in its midst and to respond to it. Such a reading of the Bible reopens the story of salvation instead of treating it as a finished outline about which listeners can only be informed and persuaded. Preaching that follows the model of Joshua, Jeremiah, Nehemiah, and Jesus and reads Scripture in this way will sound quite different from much of the preaching we currently hear. It will not threaten hell or promise heaven, and it will not serve as a booster for any particular institution. Freed from these demands, it can become a vehicle to remind listeners of their ability to choose to ally themselves with God's redeeming work in personal, local, national, and global arenas. These choices might not involve activities that serve principally to maintain the institutional church. Before that day can come, however, we need to be realistic about the patterns of institutional Christianity that will work against such preaching.

Obstacles to a Missional Reading of Scripture

I have used the passages we've just examined many times in classes on missional preaching, asking various class members to read them aloud. When seminarians and clergy give voice to these Scriptures, I am struck by the consistently monotonous tone they employ. They're intelligent, articulate people, sometimes gifted with lovely speaking voices, but some other aspect of their formation kicks in when they're asked to read the Bible aloud. Perhaps if they were asked to read the same passages in church on Sunday morning they would offer them with more urgency, while a classroom setting doesn't invite that kind of investment. But I think what is really going on is that their education has taught them to think of Scripture as stories about the ancient past, and individual passages are simply so many dead butterflies pinned in a case— beautiful once but lifeless now. And the monotony I've heard again and again in the voices of future and present preachers who read Scripture aloud cannot be improved by offering the readings more "dramatically." Exaggerated emphasis and melodramatic reenactments simply reinforce the sense of Scripture's irrelevance, making it twitch like a dead frog's leg jolted with electricity. Only when we believe that a missional God is still sending those who choose to live under the reign of God into a world that needs reconciliation and healing can we hear and read the Scriptures in a new voice.

Thinking of the Scripture as an artifact of a lost time is one impediment to reading it missionally, but so are the liturgical year and the lectionary for those churches that use one or both. (Even those that do not do so "officially" are affected by their rhythms, in any case.) Take Advent, for example. Even though everyone knows that the four Sundays of the season will end with Christmas, we hear preaching every year that tries to fill listeners with a sense of anticipation, as though some outcome other than the birth of Jesus might be possible. Banners that proclaim "Only *15* Days until the King Comes!" attempt to baptize the Christmas shopping season and build a sense of excitement. Because so many people love this season and the various cultural and family practices associated with it, they may not notice that the preaching they hear is employing a rather strained hermeneutical move, speaking of things that happened long ago as though they were still in the future. This practice of preaching sermons of anticipation during Advent is as widespread as the old saw about afflicting the comfortable, and equally impossible to trace to its source. But it is *not* the kind of present-tense immediacy of the scriptural story that I've been speaking of in this chapter. Instead of asking where a missional God is sending the assembly of the baptized as another year draws to its close, it encourages the congregation to imagine itself living in the past, preparing for a long-ago event to happen again and again. At some point the liturgical year begins to look like the movie *Groundhog Day* with Bill Murray, forcing its participants to relive the same events until they get them right. It's no surprise that attendance begins to wane in most churches after Easter, when nothing of the story of Jesus is left to "relive" and the church must tell its own story.

Preaching out of a missional understanding of the Scriptures requires big-picture thinking, something we've seen above in the "preaching" of Joshua, Jeremiah, Nehemiah, and Jesus. These speakers place their listeners in the context of a great history and invite them to write its next chapter. The lectionary, however, fragments the Bible and destroys almost all sense of chronology, reinforcing the dissection approach to the Scriptures most clergy were taught in seminary. I am full of admiration for the scholars who produced the lectionaries of the twentieth century. Both the Common and the Revised Common Lectionaries accomplish the goal of ensuring that a great deal of the Bible is read publicly in the community of faith over a period of three years, and they organize the readings within those three years in systematic and helpful ways. But a coherent sense of God's actions in history leading up to the present moment is difficult to achieve using only the Scriptures assigned by the lectionary. To see the reign of God being offered again and again in human history we need a wide-angle lens, not a microscope. Preachers who reimagine the Scriptures using an outline like that on pages 88–89 above and who consistently ask the assembly to join them in discerning what shape God's mission is taking in the present day and in their specific context can begin to break out of the mold of sermons intended to maintain an institution and swell its membership. Preachers can also let go of at least some of their anxiety about saving souls or changing the world. Their reconceived task is to proclaim the reign of God in a way that listeners can grasp it and freely choose it as gift. When the preachers have done that, they're finished. The result is no longer up to them. They no longer have to worry about "pushing God's message across."

CHAPTER 7

Crafting and Preaching the Missional Sermon

If you've gotten this far, you are surely wondering how to turn all this history and argument into weekly sermons. It's surprisingly easy; in fact, I give my classes a handout that provides a step-by-step guide to producing missional sermons. You might then ask, why not just start there, with the "how to"? The reason is simple. Without the background we've built up in the earlier chapters of this book, the step-by-step guide would make no sense. Not because the language is opaque or full of insider jargon but because you would inevitably bring a maintenance or Christendom perspective to the outline that would produce sermons that differ little from your current ones. It's been my experience that preachers need to undergo a process of *metanoia*, of "changing their minds," to think about the kingdom of God, the congregation, and the Scripture differently than they have in the past. When that change begins to take root, they inevitably progress quickly and can soon tell me a thing or two about how best to put all this into practice. But they still tell me that the step-by-step guide is helpful, even if they no longer use it, or do it differently themselves now.

Begin with Ourselves

Before we can preach the kingdom of God to anyone else, we need to know what we think about it ourselves. Ask yourself the questions I introduced in chapter 4. What does the kingdom of God look like for you? Here's the Jack Nelson-Pallmeyer quote once again to help you:

> The kingdom of God is present on earth whenever life accurately reflects the will and sovereignty of God. It is the way life and society would be if a compassionate God were in charge or imitated instead of Roman governors, client kings, and the Temple establishment.[1]

When you think of the kingdom that way, how will it show up in your personal life? What about in your home life? In your parish community? In your city, your state, your nation? Where do you find the kingdom of God on the global scene? Take pen and paper or sit at the computer and start making lists of your responses to these various levels of imagination. Remember to *be specific* rather than general. Use names, visual details, smells, and sounds to make the kingdom live in your heart and mind. If Jesus could say that the kingdom of heaven is like ten bridesmaids with varying degrees of oil in their lamps, can you say that the kingdom of God is like your teenage son dressed in his tux and ready for his first prom with a spot of ketchup he can't see on his lapel? If Jesus can say the kingdom of heaven is like herds of sheep and goats gathered before a royal throne, can you compare it to the moment when thousands of athletes gathered in the sweltering heat of Chicago's Soldier Field for the opening of the 2006 Gay Games, many having come at the risk of their lives, and collectively illuminated a rainbow flag with glowsticks in the summer night?[2] While these examples might seem particular to the point of solipsism, it has been my experience and that of my students that such specificity comes as a blessed relief from the vague platitudes heard in many sermons. The vividness of the description awakens the imagination of listeners to see and feel the presence of the kingdom in new and startling ways. My friend Yushi Nomura, a Christian minister and artist, once told a story about staying home sick from school in his native Japan. At the end of the afternoon he poked little holes in the rice-paper walls of his room to watch his classmates laughing and talking as they made their way home. When you offer specific details about where you see the reign of God present in the world, you poke a little hole in the wall of everyday experience and offer people a glimpse of a divine reality that has always been there but had never been seen till you described it.

If you are accustomed to beginning your sermon preparation by reading lots of commentaries, you may find this approach difficult, even suspect. In chapter 4 I made a passing reference to using your intuitive and associative mind rather than your cognitive and analytical one. I'd like to say more about that now. I am indebted to Viriginia Wiles, professor of New Testament at New Brunswick Theological Seminary, for introducing me to this helpful way of thinking about the distinction.

At a preaching conference for Episcopal seminarians in June 2006, I heard Professor Wiles quote from two essays by Virginia Woolf on the subject of reading. In the first, "Hours in the Library," Woolf distinguishes two types of readers: people who love reading and people who love learning. Wiles suggested that seminaries tend to require students to become learners rather than readers, approaching texts—even scriptural texts—for what can be gleaned from them for some other use, whether an exegesis paper or a sermon. When such reading is done in a systematic way and the insights are recorded, the result is a Scripture commentary. A second Woolf essay, "How Should One Read a Book?" offers a maxim that might be hard for those schooled in the necessity of beginning with such commentaries to stomach: "Take no advice . . . follow your own instincts . . . use your own reason . . . come to your own conclusions. Do not dictate to your author; try to become him."[3] Wiles's message to the seminarians was neither anti-intellectual nor lackadaisical. She argued not for the abolition of analysis and interpretation but for the awakening and strengthening of the underdeveloped portions of our brain that are capable of reading for the love of it, letting texts speak to us in as unencumbered a way as may be possible given our years of training in a different kind of reading, and trusting our associative minds to allow us to know those texts in alternate but equally valid ways. "We need to teach the text so students will fall in love with it," Wiles said. "Only out of that love are sermons born." It is not a question of substituting one approach for another but of complementing an overdeveloped approach with new skills from an underdeveloped one.

Of course, Wiles was speaking of how we might approach the reading of scriptural texts for preaching, whether those texts be assigned by the lectionary or freely chosen. But this exercise in imagining the kingdom of God is a good place to start honing our abilities to know through association rather than through analysis. If you find it unproductive simply to ask yourself about the kingdom at the personal through the global level, take a cluster of scriptural images of the reign of God and try the exercise on those. (A reminder: they're already gathered for you in chapter 4.) You will most likely find that some speak directly to your personal life while others remind you of something you've seen on the news that day. Instead of rushing to find out what these images "mean" and how they might have functioned in their original context (as if we can ever know precisely either the context or how they functioned in it!), see what they reveal to you about the nature and direction of God's reign among us.

As I mentioned in chapter 4, when preachers first undertake this kind of exercise to awaken their imaginations to the presence of the kingdom of God, their lists of responses tend to look like "a few of my favorite things" from *The Sound of Music* ("Raindrops on roses and whiskers on kittens . . ."). There are several correctives to this natural tendency toward the Hallmark in all of us. One is to imagine the kingdom not only on the personal and parish levels but on the national and global levels as well. A second is to use a guiding quote like Nelson-Pallmeyer's, which removes us from the realm of sentiment and reminds us how much the proclamation of the kingdom cost Jesus himself. A third is to involve the entire parish community in the project of picturing the kingdom. One parish pastor who took my class in 2006 decided to invite the whole congregation to engage in the exercise. A series of workshops led to the placement of placards around the church and grounds in unexpected locations with the words "The kingdom of God is like . . ." or "We know the reign of God is near us when . . ." followed by a parishioner's particular idea, sometimes accompanied by a picture. She noticed that after an initial burst of poetry and "a few of my favorite things" kinds of responses, the imagery of the kingdom quickly opened out into pictures of mission particular to that community and the actual circumstances of its surrounding city.

Claiming Our Own Agency

Once we've begun to generate specific ideas and images about the kingdom of God that don't describe a place we go when we die or the expansion of the institutional church and its activities, we need to ask ourselves where our own agency as preachers resides. Before you can preach agency to others, you have to be able to name it for yourself. This question puts our finger on a hot-button issue, however. I have argued in this book that the institutional church has created a system in which clergy appear to have the greatest agency of anyone in the Christian community, especially in worship. We wear the special clothes or vestments, we conduct the liturgy, we preach the sermons, and we set (or try to set) the direction for the parish community's life and witness. But it's been my experience that clergy rarely feel as empowered as others perceive us to be. Many of us feel constrained by our societal role or by denominational or parish expectations. The impulse to follow Jesus that led us into professional ministry may have long since been submerged by the rigors of seminary, the obstacle course of the ordination process, and the demands of running an organization. When do we have the chance to ask whether we ourselves are choosing the reign of God each day and year of our lives? And are we able to sort out the choice for the kingdom from the exercise of our jobs?

Michael Warren's book *At This Time, In This Place*, cited in chapter 5, does not specifically address the choice for the reign of God, but in his discussion of "How We Speak in Church," Warren provides a helpful set of questions that can enable preachers to sort out what we have power to do:

How do clergy view themselves in relation to the speech of the community:

As the voice of the assembly?

As a voice within the assembly?

As the facilitator of the varied voices within the assembly?

As a facilitator helping the assembly discover its common judgment?[4]

Warren is asking clergy to examine all their public and private speaking in their official capacity, not just preaching; but the questions are a way to surface what we believe we're doing as preachers. Understanding ourselves as "the voice of the assembly" is probably the most common reality for those who give sermons. After all, when preachers speak, everyone else listens, and when they say "we," there is little opportunity for any individual member of the assembly to object. Clergy striving—sincerely or insincerely—to appear more modest may identify themselves as simply "a voice *within* the assembly," but the weight of institutional power can make this claim seem disingenuous. Allowing "varied voices within the assembly" to be heard may seem more appropriate to a parish council meeting than to preaching, while "helping the assembly discover its common judgment" may seem an impossible task, given the spectrum of opinions found in most congregations. Yet Warren's fourth possibility is in fact the goal of missional preaching. Recall the New Testament model presented in chapter 3: the first preachers sent by Jesus proclaimed the kingdom, demonstrated its power through acts of healing, and then moved on. They did not inform and then persuade; they proclaimed and then allowed their listeners to respond. Warren's fourth possibility for the exercise of preachers' voices is most like that New Testament model: speech that precipitates *crisis*, judgment, and then releases the listener to act on the truth discerned.

Thinking about sermons in this way has proved to be the second biggest revelation for seasoned preachers. (The first is the realization that the kingdom of God comes as gift and can only be received or entered, not built or extended.) Most clergy want to do more than simply preach good sermons; they also feel responsible for their listeners' taking those sermons to heart and acting on them. Missional preaching absolves us of that worry. While missional preachers certainly have to make every effort to proclaim the kingdom *clearly,* their responsibility ends with that clarity. It's been my experience that giving preachers permission to let go of the results of their sermons leads to greater integrity, creativity, power, and love in their preaching rather than the "take it or leave it" attitude that you'd imagine might be the result of such permission. But it is such a different way of thinking about preaching that missional preachers require a new model of sermon preparation to achieve different results. As with so many transitions in life, achieving that model means letting go of one way of thinking and taking up another.

Letting Go of Exegesis/Illustration/Application

Many of us were taught to compose sermons using some version of this process: first, do the exegesis, working from the original scriptural language if you know it. Second, find a contemporary illustration of the key idea or ideas your exegesis has presented you with. Finally, give a concrete application of the sermon's main idea, so that listeners will know how to put your sermon into practice in their daily lives. I'd like to develop this universal formula a bit more fully and explain why I believe it can never produce anything except sermons for maintenance, however heartfelt and erudite they may be.

That most Christian preaching, across centuries and denominational divisions, begins with and returns to the Scriptures of the Old and New Testaments is beyond question. Lectionary-based churches expect preachers to respond to assigned texts while non-lectionary preachers freely choose their Scripture passages, but both groups find the fountainhead of their sermons' meaning as well as their authority in the written Word of the Bible. When preachers rely too heavily on the movie they've just seen or the novel they've just read, listeners notice, usually with disapproval. But this broad agreement about how Christian preaching begins breaks down when we look at denominational and personal approaches to working with the Scriptures to produce a sermon. Some denominations require their seminarians to learn one or both of the biblical languages; others stress that the purpose of preaching is to convey doctrine to the faithful, even in cases where the biblical support for that doctrine might be slender. Free-church traditions stress the need for the preacher to offer a Spirit-filled interpretation of the biblical text independent of what others may have said about it. Who is to say which is the "right" method of reading Scripture in preparation for preaching?

What unites the preachers of mainline denominations in Europe and North America is without doubt the influence of the nineteenth-century German university, where the historical-critical study of the Bible first arose. Because of this influence on twentieth- and twenty-first-century seminary faculties and their pedagogy, many preachers turn to their Bible commentaries as the first step toward a Sunday sermon. It was not always thus. For much of Christian history the methods of reading Scripture were fourfold, ranging from the literal (what the text plainly says) to the moral (what the text asks us to do) to the allegorical (the text's hidden meaning) to the anagogical (the text as the springboard into mystical union with God). Though this taxonomy varies from century to century and across cultures, its variety of approaches is fundamentally creative and democratic. Anyone can read the Bible on these levels, even without seminary training. Nevertheless, these approaches to Scripture have produced some of the great benchmarks of Christian preaching, from Clement of Alexandria to Bernard of Clairvaux to Cotton Mather to Joel Osteen. As the body of Christian scriptural commentary grew through the years, preachers certainly availed themselves of the wisdom of their predecessors, but none felt so constrained that he or she did not feel free to add a new interpretation to the storehouse. Indeed, prior to the nineteenth century the tenor of Christian commentary on the Bible was far more like that of the rabbis the church once debated and denounced: a conversation among equals. Since the nineteenth century we have witnessed the professionalization of biblical scholarship and the development of a guild whose sole purpose is to determine the most accurate possible interpretation of the Old and New Testaments using a variety of ostensibly scientific methods. Certainly, the plethora of information about archeology, geography, history, and language available to us today can be invaluable for anyone who wants to read the Bible with greater understanding. But to the extent that a preacher feels deprived of the authority to read and interpret Scripture without a commentary we find ourselves in a new ballpark in the history of Christian preaching. The relationship of preacher to Scripture has for many become dependent on an intermediary—the commentary—to tell the preacher what the biblical text means. And most of those commentaries (with notable exceptions proliferating in the present day) share an unexamined assumption of Christianity as a worldwide institution dominated by European modes of thinking. The information contained in commentaries is neither wrong nor misguided, but it is culturally biased and written to reinforce the idea that the work of God in history is essentially completed and thus available for definitive comment.

Whenever I make such an assertion in a classroom or workshop setting, the anxiety in the room immediately rises and the pushback begins. Someone may accuse me of being anti-intellectual or pietistic. Those who know I have a Ph.D. earned by writing about the Greek text of the Gospel of John may simply be confused. The only explanation I can offer is this: the recovery of a New Testament missiology in our day is forcing us to rethink everything we've said and done within the framework of Christendom. Commentaries weren't written to support missional sermons; they were written to support and maintain two different institutions: the organized church and the religious academy. They are not pernicious or benighted; some are brilliant. But their information can help us only when we've already undergone the *metanoia* of reading the Scriptures as testimony to a missionary God who continues to send individuals and communities to proclaim God's reign and to heal whatever is broken in its absence.

Now for the second step of the conventional model of sermon preparation. Most preachers were taught to follow the exposition of their exegesis with an "illustration" to make the exegesis vivid and relevant to the contemporary listener. Here is where the movies and novels tend to creep in. A preacher's mind will be so filled with some recent stimulus from the cinema or bookshelf that she reads the scriptural passage searching for some possible connection. The balance of authority subtly shifts, and soon the biblical text is supporting the truth that the director, actor, or writer so powerfully conveyed to the preacher during the past week. For listeners who have seen the movie or read the book, such sermons can often be electrifying, confirming the deeper truth that they had also derived from their experience. Those who didn't see the movie or read the book will tend to feel left out in the cold, wondering what happened to the Bible. But even when this imbalance does not occur, when the illustration is apt and vivid, I find that the result can hardly avoid becoming a tautology: John the Baptist preaching in the wilderness is like the crazy guy down on State Street with a microphone in a briefcase, and the crazy guy down on State Street with a microphone in a briefcase is like John the Baptist preaching in the wilderness. Listeners may actually be pleased to have a contemporary example of an ancient character or event, but what has been accomplished? Is the biblical text so hopelessly out of date that only when it is given a present-day analogy does it have meaning? And is the street preacher "like" John the Baptist in any but the most superficial ways? Has he been sent to prepare the way for the Christ? An outstanding preacher can sometimes move deeply enough into the illustration to make it illuminate the biblical text, but most often the method used is that of hanging wallpaper: glue a strip to the wall, then a matching strip next to it, then stand back and admire your work; maybe hang a picture on it.

Because the illustration so often merely updates the information gained from the exegesis, a third component becomes necessary for the sermon to become truly effective: the application. From the first time this word was presented to me in the context of sermon preparation until now, I have taken exception to it. Sunscreen and mayonnaise are things that can be applied; to "apply" the Word of God to our lives has always sounded topical at best, irreverent at worst. Yet congregations everywhere cry out for it, and homiletics professors regularly teach it—this in spite of the fact that Jesus in the memory of the church repeatedly refused to answer the question of how his teaching "applied" to his listeners. Again and again, Jesus turned such questions back to the asker: "What do you think? What do you read there? What is written in the Scripture?" Of course, Jesus's successors in the New Testament overcame their Lord's reticence to give advice; Paul is a virtual "Dear Abby" of the ancient Mediterranean world. But preachers who supply the "application" for their listeners have once again robbed them of agency, the power to put on their own sunscreen or to make their own sandwiches.

Embracing Proclamation/Implication/Invitation

The preparation of missional sermons requires a process different from the one conventionally taught in seminaries. You won't need to let your commentaries gather dust, but you won't rush to find them as you begin your sermon preparation, either. Your first step will be to promise yourself never to use the word *missional* in a sermon, or at least not until you're confident that you have begun to preach missionally. That may sound like an odd suggestion from the author of a book on missional preaching, but it is far too easy for preachers to substitute talk *about* missionality for missionality itself. Missional preaching is about proclaiming the kingdom of God and healing. As Matthew's Jesus says, "Every good tree bears good fruit." It doesn't need to explain that it's a good tree!

In place of talking about the sea change in missiology, here's a different model of sermon preparation that is true to the paradigm I've been constructing throughout this book. In place of the exegesis/illustration/application model familiar to us all, I suggest *proclamation, implication,* and *invitation.* However, unlike the earlier model, these elements are not intended to be a formula for both writing and delivery; rather, they may be combined in any order or disappear into a narrative form that includes them all. This model is intended to surface a different kind of *content*, not to serve as a formula for the final architecture of the sermon. Listeners would soon tire of sermons that followed the same pattern week after week.

After we've promised ourselves not to use the word "missional," we need to get past any negative associations we have for the word "proclamation." Remember from the discussion in the third chapter of this book that "proclaim" is one of several English words used to translate the Greek verb *keryssein*.[5] In other contexts the NRSV uses "announce," "cry out," and "preach." "Announce" is probably closest to what we need for missional preaching, but it has been permanently co-opted by the "announcements" that are everyone's favorite part of the worship experience. "Cry out" sounds more like something we do when we stub our toes, and "preach" is a singularly uninspired direction to preachers. The problem with "proclamation" is that it calls to mind men in tights with trumpets and scrolls, or perhaps the annual declaration that the last Thursday in November shall be observed as Thanksgiving Day throughout the United States. The word is almost indelibly linked with power and government in our minds. That's actually not such a bad thing for our purposes, however. The purpose of missional preaching is, first and foremost, to proclaim an alternate form of government and a different source of power, not simply the vague rubber stamp upon the existing government asserted by our coins and folding money. That proclamation may take the form of a declarative statement, as it does so often in the New Testament ("The kingdom of heaven is like a mustard seed that someone took and sowed in his field . . .") or it may take the form of a story told so vividly that the outlines of the reign of God become present through it ("There was a man who had two sons . . ."). It may come at the beginning of the sermon, provide a surprise ending, or simply serve as the cumulative effect of the whole. The essential thing is that a proclamation is made, that an alternative world is announced every time the preacher opens her mouth—a world to which the listeners can give their allegiance or withhold it.

Then what? What is the listener to do with or about that proclamation? If the kingdom of heaven is like a mustard seed that someone sowed in a field, what do we actually know about it? Here the preacher would typically move on to illustration, helping listeners to grasp Jesus's obscure language. The trouble is, once we've "illustrated" the original, it is no longer the same thing, often lacking the unique power it once had. We can learn from Jesus, however, to tease out the implications of the proclamation using its own terms: "[The mustard seed] is the smallest of all the seeds, but when it has grown it is the greatest of shrubs and becomes a tree, so that the birds of the air come and make nests in its branches" (Matt. 13:31-32). Even with these additions, do we know any more than we did before? Have these amplifying words "illustrated" the proclamation? Not really, but our minds are working now. We are turning the proclamation over and looking at it from several directions, trying to see what it might be or do. The specificity of it intrigues us, even as we wonder what it might correspond to in our world of death and taxes.

The parable of the mustard seed is a good one to illustrate this approach, because it has become a favorite of preachers even while its more radical implications have been suppressed. Just as the exegetes of the Middle Ages conflated all the Marys of the New Testament (other than the mother of Jesus) into a single character, so preachers of the past two hundred years have conflated Jesus's several references to mustard seeds into a kind of "mustard-seed theology" that proclaims Small Is Good. Who has not heard a sermon about the miraculous effects that can be achieved from even the smallest amount of faith? By and large, these sermons are addressed not to communities but to individuals who happen to be sitting next to one another in church, encouraging each of them in his or her private realm to have faith to achieve seemingly impossible goals. The popularity of the message is evidenced by the vast numbers of mustard-seed necklaces that have been sold since pourable resin was invented. (An Internet search for such jewelry yielded 90,800 results.) It's fairly easy to see why a message of believing the impossible might appeal to the contrarian economy of the Christian religion—the last first, the least the greatest, and so on. Yet what has become the dominant form of "mustard-seed theology" is based on only one use of the image, that of Matthew 17:20 and Luke 17:6, where Jesus says we need faith only the size of a mustard seed to move mountains and mulberry trees. In Matthew 13:31-32, Mark 4:30-31, and Luke 13:18-19, the mustard seed describes not faith but the reign of God. If these parables are interpreted on the level of personal piety and the aspirations of individuals, they no longer make sense. In Mark and Luke, Jesus asks: "What is the kingdom of God like?" The answer is a mustard seed that becomes a great shrub. Matthew's Jesus categorically states: *"The kingdom of heaven is like a mustard seed that someone took and planted."* So here it's not just about how small the seed is but about someone's doing something with it. What if the sown mustard seed is the proclamation of God's reign planted in human history, producing, when it takes root, a society of true hospitality upon the earth? Not a great empire, which might have been imaged as a mighty tree (as it is elsewhere in Scripture), and not a worldwide institution like organized Christianity, but simply a big *shrub* where lots of different birds find a home—serviceable, but hardly awe-inspiring.

Thinking about a familiar parable in this way is an example of *implication* rather than illustration. Using the terms of the proclamation itself, we turn it around to see how we might be implicated in its meaning, like the cast members of a *film noir* who try to figure out who is implicated by the facts of a crime. Missional preaching asks, "If *this*, then what about *this*?" If the kingdom of heaven is like a mustard seed, who plants it? What does that planting look like for the community listening to this sermon? What might the great shrub mean for us, in our time and place, and what birds of the air are seeking its shelter? The use of implication rather than illustration honors the assembly's agency, inviting listeners' shared discernment about the meaning of the proclamation of God's reign rather than simply telling them how to interpret it. For this practice to become fully effective, however, the missional sermon needs to become dialogical, either during the act of preaching itself or through opportunities following worship, in study and ministry group meetings, or in online parish blogs. For that ongoing discernment to begin, the missional sermon has to have a strong sense of *invitation*.

Invitation has a nice, gentle sound. We love getting invitations to parties, showers, and weddings, often because we know we will be entertained at someone else's expense. The invitation to participate in the reign of God, by contrast, seems harsh and almost defiant: "Let anyone with ears to hear listen!" (Matt. 11:13, 13:9, many others). "Even the dust of your town that clings to our feet, we wipe off in protest against you. Yet know this: the kingdom of God has come near" (Luke 10:16). In spite of the confrontational tone of these words, the truest invitation may be the one we have to decide whether to accept, knowing that our acceptance will require something of us beyond simply being entertained. *Invitation* differs significantly from application because it requires the listener to come to some judgment about whether she will receive the reign of God, whether he will choose to live according to its precepts.

And so we come full circle to the "crisis" with which this book opened, understanding it now as the perpetually available choice afforded human beings to discern the action of God in history and choose to embrace it or walk away from it. Missional preaching, the preaching of the crisis/*krisis* of the reign of God come near to us, brings us by any number of paths—arresting story, prophetic oracle, surprising commentary—to that moment when the rubber hits the road: God's reign on earth is here, right beside you, for the choosing: do you want it or not? In an ideal world of neat suburban lawns and picket fences, the question may sound off-putting, its advantages unclear. But offer that same choice in the Austin neighborhood of Chicago, 7.6 square miles of the city with both the highest concentration of churches and the highest number of gun-related deaths each year, and you will not only get takers—they will know what their choice means for them. Make it in Belfast, Lebanon, or East Timor—all places where Christians face conflict among themselves or with other societal groups—and the same proclamation of the kingdom of God will implicate its listeners differently and invite them to different forms of resistance and renewal.[6] The wager of this book is that the proclamation is not different for different cultural and socioeconomic groups: it's always the same, but how each group receives and enters the reign of God will look different. Do the listeners themselves need to change, or do they need to work together to change their conditions and make them permeable to the reign of God? The missional sermon's invitation is not to accept an idea but to adopt a *practice*, one that the preacher intends to implement herself, one that will enable preacher and assembly together to enter the reign of God more fully and to live its healing practices more faithfully.

Sweat the Big Stuff, Pay Attention to the Small Stuff

Still wondering how to begin? Let's start with the small stuff. Whether you have a text assigned to you by the lectionary or the

Spirit has moved you to select one freely, go through that text and highlight the words and phrases that point to:

- The missional nature of God: what aspect of God's sending does this story point to?
- The presence of the kingdom of God.
- The need for renewal or resistance.
- Potential practices that derive from the text.
- Agency: who acts in this story, what is their motivation, and what is the result?

Next, contextualize your passage in a missional paradigm:

- Where does this passage occur in the history of God's sending?
- How is God's reign being advanced or impeded in this passage?
- If the kingdom of God is like this passage, who is implicated by it?
- Where might the aspect of the kingdom you find in this passage be found in your own life, or that of your church community, your city, your nation, or the world?

Now, craft an opening sentence that proclaims the kingdom of God in such a way that *you* feel intrigued, invited, or challenged. Remember to use specific ideas and images, not abstract theology-speak. ("The reign of God is like employees and managers of our local big-box store sitting on the church steps playing cards," and not "The reign of God calls us all to be good stewards.") Put that sentence in places where you'll run into it throughout the week. Fold it up and place it in your pocket or your purse when you go about your work. Read the newspaper, watch television, and read commentaries with your sentence in mind. Allow your sermon to grow organically from the proclamation you've crafted. Who is implicated by it? What practices does it commend? Bear in mind that "practices" are not the same as "projects." If your text leads you to the inescapable conclusion that embracing the reign of God in your town means not letting anyone go hungry and you propose creating a food pantry as your response, you can't just move on to a new need and a new response the next week. If your food pantry is truly to be a sign of God's reign come near, you might want to put many other practices in place before and after its creation: the practice of noticing the difficult choices the young mother ahead of you in the grocery-store line is forced to make; the practice of looking at the food on your own table and feeling not just grateful but empowered by your abundance; the practice of asking what other kinds of "food" might be needed for healing and reconciliation in your town.

The big stuff is not properly the subject of any one sermon but the overall context in which we begin to preach missionally, as we gradually loosen the hold our seminary education had on us and find new ways to use the skills and knowledge we acquired there to enter the Bible and Christian story. We need to ask ourselves these questions again and again: Do we believe that human history is open or closed? Is the kingdom of God still at hand for us to choose? Is God's mission accomplished or ongoing? Seminary taught us that it's all pretty much a done deal—just tell people about it and help them see why they should care. You can't undo that kind of formation overnight, but if you're willing to recognize a framework of interpretation for what it is, you can put it down and try another one without feeling that you've wasted three years of time and tuition. There was probably a great deal of excellence and wisdom in the seminary education you received, but the paradigm that gave rise to it and the church it was created to serve are both rapidly receding into history. It's time to ask new questions of ourselves, our listeners, and the sacred text.

Changing Your Expectations for a Response

Because so much of our preaching is offered with the hopes and fears of participants in a talent show, preachers often approach the awarding of their "scores" at the church door or the coffee hour with these questions in their minds: "How was I today? Did you like it? Do you like me? Do you like me more than you did before? Are you angry with me? Will you still give your money anyway?" None of us wants these questions to be at the forefront of our gracious encounters with parishioners, but they circulate in our brains nonetheless. Learning to preach missionally is a kind of exorcism of those voices, gradually bidding them to be silent so that more significant questions can be asked: "Did you hear the kingdom of God proclaimed today? Do you see how both my life and yours are implicated by it? Do you feel invited to embrace the reign of God, no matter how difficult? What can you add to what you heard? I'd really like to know." These questions, too, ought to remain unheard, but they can coach us to look for different responses that are less about us and more about the action of God in our midst.

After all, if we really embrace the apostolic model of being sent to proclaim the kingdom of God and to heal, if we understand that once we've truly proclaimed the kingdom the response is beyond our control, then we should begin to expect not a scorecard for our efforts but the range of reactions Jesus and the apostles themselves elicited by their own preaching of the reign of God and its privileges and demands. Some heard the message with joy; others went away shocked and sorrowful. Those Jesus trained and sent as his first missional preachers were amazed that it "worked": "'Whoever listens to you listens to me, and whoever rejects you rejects me, and whoever rejects me rejects the one who sent me.' The seventy returned with joy, saying, 'Lord, in your name even the demons submit to us!'" (Luke 10:16-17). Jesus's response to those first "sent ones" remains a cautionary note for preachers who hope that missional preaching will "work" for them as well: "Do not rejoice at this, that the spirits submit to you, but rejoice that your names are written in heaven" (Luke 10:20).

A Word of Encouragement

Finally, a word of encouragement: don't worry about getting it right. Missional preaching is a long-term proposition—the gradual introduction of images, attitudes, and language that work against more than a millennium of preaching that equated the kingdom of God with the afterlife or the organized church. In time, missional sermons can shape missional communities, and the practices of those communities will in turn shape the preaching that is offered in their midst. If you are focused on choosing the kingdom and fostering agency in the congregation, your preaching will shift over time. The weight of that shift doesn't rest on any one sermon. As one of my doctoral students wrote in a reflection paper for a course on missional preaching, "If, in fact, the reign of God is here and still to come, it stands to reason that not only are we ourselves to receive it and enter it, but we need to allow ourselves to be so shaped by it that it becomes the reality out of which we live."[7] A tall order, as Jesus knew. Perhaps that's why he discouraged halfway measures. "No one who puts a hand to the plow and looks back is fit for the kingdom of God," he said to a potential follower. As we move forward, eagerly or filled with misgivings, into a post-Christendom, post-maintenance future, Jesus's words to the other potential follower in that passage from Luke become all the more poignant to our ears: "Let the dead bury their own dead; but as for you, go and proclaim the kingdom of God" (Luke 9:60).

Notes

Chapter 1

1. *www.askoxford.com*

2. San Francisco: Jossey-Bass, 2004, 10.

3. This book is cited by Anthony Bradley on his blog, *http://anthonybradley.worldmagblog.com (anthonybradley/archives/024531.html);* it is listed as out of print by Amazon.com and has not surfaced in a search of online library catalogues.

4. New York: Fleming H. Revell Co., 1919.

5. Darrell Guder et al., *Missional Church: A Vision for the Sending of the Church in North America* (Grand Rapids: Eerdmans, 1998).

6. A fuller description of the Gospel and Our Culture Network follows. See also *www.gocn.org*

7. Guder et al., *Missional Church,* 4, 6.

8. Hubert J. B. Allen, *Roland Allen: Pioneer, Priest and Prophet* (Grand Rapids: Eerdmans, 1995).

9. Harvie M. Conn, "The Missionary Task of Theology: A Love-Hate Relationship?," *Westminster Theological Journal* 45:13; quoted in Bosch, *Transforming Mission,* 494.

10. Douglas John Hall, *The Reality of the Gospel and the Unreality of the Churches (Philadelphia:* Westminster Press, 1975), 79-80.

11. Cardinal Joseph Ratzinger was elected pope and took the name Benedict XVI on April 19, 2005.

12. For the former, see John 9:39, 12:31, 16:11; 2 Thessalonians 1:5; 1 Peter 4:17; for the latter, see Matthew 5:21, Luke 10:14, James 2:13, 2 Peter 2:9.

13. "For we know, brothers and sisters beloved by God, that he has chosen you, because our message of the gospel came to you not in word only, but also in power and in the Holy Spirit and with full conviction. . . . And you became imitators of us and of the Lord, for in spite of persecution you received the word with joy inspired by the Holy Spirit, so that you became an example to all the believers in Macedonia and in Achaia" (1 Thess. 1:4-7).

14. Paul Tillich, *Theology of Culture* (New York: Oxford University Press, 1959), 213.

15. Hall, *Reality of the Gospel,* 82 ff.

Chapter 2

1. For a good summary of this trend, see Craig L. Nessan, *Beyond Maintenance to Mission: A Theology of the Congregation* (Minneapolis: Augsburg Fortress, 1999).

2. Howard Hanchey, *From Survival to Celebration: Leadership for the Confident Church* (Boston: Cowley Press, 1994).

3. Hanchey, *From Survival to Celebration,* 90-91.

4. Recounted in Judy Rois, *Luke Is Not My Husband* (Seabury-Western Theological Seminary D.Min. in Preaching thesis, unpublished, 2006).

Chapter 3

1. Latin verbs are typically displayed this way to show the possible variations of their forms: *present active indicative, present active infinitive, perfect active indicative,* and *perfect passive participle*: I send, to send, I sent, sent. "Mission" comes from the perfect passive participle.

2. See, for instance, Matthew 24:14, Mark 1:39, Acts 10:42, Romans 2:21, Galatians 5:11.

3. I am well aware that many readers may want to protest that they do, in fact, feel "sent by Jesus" in their preaching ministries. I would like to think that such a conviction is out there, but the overwhelming experience of those coming through my classrooms from the full spectrum of denominations has not yet reflected it.

4. Richard A. Horsley and Neil Asher Silberman, *The Message and the Kingdom: How Jesus and Paul Ignited a Revolution and Transformed the Ancient World* (New York: Grosset/Putnam, 1997), 10, 51.

5. Horsley and Silberman, *The Message and the Kingdom*, 54-58.

6. John Dominic Crossan, *The Historical Jesus: The Life of a Mediterranean Jewish Peasant* (San Francisco: HarperSanFrancisco, 1991), 324.

7. Crossan, *The Historical Jesus*, 341.

Chapter 4

1. *The Book of Common Prayer* (1976), according to the use of the Episcopal Church (New York: Church Hymnal Corp. and Seabury Press, 1977), 387, 389, 393.

2. Ibid., 205.

3. Ibid., 196.

4. *The Constitution of the Presbyterian Church (USA): Part 2: Book of Order 2007-2008* (Louisville: Office of the General Assembly, 2007), G-10100, "1. The Head of the Church"; *www.pcusa.org/oga/consti/fog/index.htm*.

5. The word "kingdom" does occur additional times in the New Testament. These tabulations refer to the use of "kingdom of God" or "kingdom of heaven" and to the phrase "your kingdom come" in the Lord's Prayer.

6. Jack Nelson-Pallmeyer, *Jesus against Christianity* (Harrisburg, Pa.: Trinity Press International), 17.

7. Horsley and Silberman, *The Message and the Kingdom*, 51.

8. Ibid., 54.

9. Ibid., 55-56.

10. Crossan, *The Historical Jesus*, 333 forward.

11. Horsley and Silberman, *The Message and the Kingdom*, 151.

12. John 2:20, Matthew 5:15, Mark 12:1, Matthew 16:18.

13. Acts 20:32, 1 Corinthians 14:4.

14. Romans 12:13.

15. 2 Corinthians 4:13.

16. Hebrews 8:8.

17. Mark 1:28, John 21:23, Acts 6:7.

18. My condensed summary of pp. 222-223 of Thomas Sheehan, *The First Coming* (New York: Random House, 1988).

19. Sheehan, *The First Coming,* 222.

20. Guder et al., *Missional Church,* 79. Guder is the overall editor of the book, but the authors of individual chapters are identified in the introduction.

21. Nelson-Pallmeyer, *Jesus against Christianity,* 17.

Chapter 5

1. Michael Warren, *At This Time, In This Place: The Spirit Embodied in the Local Assembly* (Harrisburg, Pa.: Trinity Press International, 1999), 76-77.

2. Warren, *At This Time,* 77.

3. A random search of the phrase on the Internet yielded this as the first result: "Ministerial students are taught an aphorism to keep in mind when constructing sermons: good preaching should 'comfort the afflicted, and afflict the comfortable.'" The source is a sermon preached on September 24, 2006, by the Rev. Dr. Kathy Fuson Hurt, pastor of First Baptist Church of Granville, Ohio. See Web site *www.firstbaptistgranville.org/sundaysermons?id=34244*

4. Writing a syndicated column in the persona of "Mr. Dooley," supposedly an Irish bartender on the South Side of Chicago, Dunne offered this description of the role of a newspaper in society: "Th' newspaper does ivrything f'r us. It runs th' polis foorce an' th' banks, commands th' milishy, controls th'ligislachure, baptizes th' young, marries th' foolish, comforts th' afflicted, afflicts th' comfortable, buries th' dead an' roasts thim aftherward."

5. Depending on the system used, the estimates range from 20,000 to 40,000. For a variety of answers, see *www.religioustolerance.org/worldrel.htm* or *www.bringyou.to/apologetics/a120.htm* or *www.adherents.com/*

6. Guder et al., *Missional Church,* 206.

7. Peter Brown, *The World of Late Antiquity* (London: Thames and Hudson, Ltd.; and New York: Harcourt Brace, Jovanovich 1971), 66.

8. Warren, *At This Time,* 86-87.

9. John McClure, *The Roundtable Pulpit* (Nashville: Abingdon, 1995 and 2007); and Lucy Atkinson Rose, *Sharing the Word: Preaching in the Roundtable Church* (Louisville: Westminster John Knox, 1997).

Chapter 6

1. Bosch was writing in 1990.

2. David Bosch, *Transforming Mission: Paradigm Shifts in Theology of Mission* (Maryknoll, N.Y.: Orbis Books, 1991), 389-390.

3. The proper name for this festival is actually Shemini Atzeret, or "Eighth [Day] of Assembly."

4. *The Madwoman of Chaillot*, film produced by Commonwealth United Entertainment, 1969; directed by Bryan Forbes; screenplay by Edward Anhalt based on Maurice Valency's adaptation of Jean Giraudoux's original 1947 stage play.

Chapter 7

1. Nelson-Pallmeyer, *Jesus against Christianity*, 17.

2. This example was suggested independently by three students during a Missional Preaching class in summer 2006.

3. Virginia Woolf, "Hours in the Library," in *The Essays of Virginia Woolf*, vol. II, 1912-1918; Andrew NcNeillie, ed. (New York: Harcourt Brace Jovanovich, 1987); and "How Should One Read a Book?" in *The Second Common Reader, Annotated Edition* (San Diego and New York: Harvest Books, an imprint of Harcourt Trade Publishers, 2003), 258.

4. Michael Warren, *At This Time, In This Place,* 98.

5. See page 29 above.

6. I am indebted to Horsley and Silbermann's *The Message and the Kingdom* for the phrase "resistance and renewal" to characterize two aspects of the response to the preaching of Jesus and Paul.

7. Hannah Anderson, Seabury Institute Integrative Paper #3, June 2005, unpublished.